THE POWER
OF AMBITION

THE POWER
OF AMBITION

AWAKENING THE POWERFUL FORCE WITHIN YOU

JIM ROHN

Published and distributed by:
SOUND WISDOM
P.O. Box 310
Shippensburg, PA 17257-0310
717-530-2122

info@soundwisdom.com

www.soundwisdom.com

Cover design by Eileen Rockwell

ISBN 13 TP: 978-1-64095-355-0

ISBN 13 eBook: 978-1-64095-356-7

For Worldwide Distribution, Printed in the U.S.A.

3 4 5 6 7 8 / 26 25 24 23

Contents

Foreword

For more than 30 years, Jim Rohn focused on the fundamentals of human behavior that led to exceptional personal and business performance. He established an unparalleled reputation as a dynamic and memorable speaker. The power behind his message is not just in what you learn by reading, but in what you feel. For that reason, he uniquely presents *The Power of Ambition.*

Throughout this book, Jim guides you to the true source of ambition, the one that resides within you. His inspirational approach will help you develop your inner motivation and drive. You will discover insights and strategies to take you to the highest levels of achievement by learning how you can harness the power of your own personal ambition.

Introduction

Ambition is a powerful force. The power of ambition turns hopeful wishes into reality. It leads you on the right course to the good life. Legitimate ambition says, "I only want something at the *service* of others, not at the *expense* of others."

If it is your ambition to be great, you must first find a way to do so by serving others. If it is your ambition to be wealthy, you must first learn how to give. If it is your ambition to be healthy, you must first learn to stop doing the things that can make you and others sick.

You're about to read why ambition is at the core of every success. I encourage you to underline important truth statements and take notes to expand relevant information presented to fit your personal plans and goals.

But remember, this book is only the beginning. The insights you will learn are seeds that have the capacity to lead to extraordinary achievement. My hope is that you will cultivate these ideas with your own imagination and creativity, water them with your faith, and intensify them with action so they will grow and bear fruit.

I'm always intrigued with the challenge of putting into words the ideas that can make a difference in a person's life. And now I have the pleasure of sharing these ideas with you.

The Mystery of Ambition

To a lot of people, ambition seems to be a mystery. The dictionary says it's "an eager desire for distinction, power, or fame," but what does that really mean? Well, let's start with the word *eager*. All by itself, *eager* is kind of exciting. Kids are eager for their birthday parties. They expect to be the center of attention, get lots of presents, eat too much. I guess grown-ups are eager for birthdays too, unless of course they're embarrassed that the number of candles on the cake outnumbers their achievements.

But we can be eager to see a ball game, eager to see our kids in a dance recital, eager to see an old friend, eager to shop for a new car. Eager sounds like a lot of fun. But do you ever hear people say they are eager to live a better life, eager to have better family relationships, eager to make a lot of money? Probably not.

And that's a problem, because how I see it, living a better life, having better family relationships, and making a lot of money takes an eager desire. We have the remarkable ability to get exactly what we must have, but there is a difference between wishes and desires.

Wishing Versus Desire

You have probably heard people say, "Oh, I wish I could drop five pounds. I want to be a little lighter." And we've probably said it ourselves, especially after a big holiday dinner of turkey and homemade pie and every other thing we can possibly stuff ourselves with in one eight-hour period of time. And even though we wish we could breathe a little easier in our clothing, we have to have the desire to exercise a little more and eat a little less. The "I *wish* I could lose weight" has to become "I have the *eager desire* to lose weight."

I'm also sure you've heard people talk about wishing they had more money to pay the bills or take a vacation or just to take a little pressure off of life. But before their lifestyle can change, their wish needs to become a desire. If they really desired change, they wouldn't spend their evenings watching TV and wishing they were doing something more.

True ambition is disciplined, eager desire.

The backbone of an eager desire to change is discipline. True ambition is disciplined, eager desire. It's that little part within us that says, "If I want to be ready for that meeting tomorrow, I need to finish preparing for it today. If I want to make sure I can pay for my kid's college education, I need to start saving today. If I want a better life tomorrow, I need to start working on it today."

Ambition is a minute-by-minute, day-by-day mentality. To have the ambition to work toward a better family life, a newer car, a bigger house, a financially secure future, you have to live it every moment. If living a successful life was easy, I'm sure more people would be successful. If just being ambitious was enough, I'm sure all of the broke and perplexed people in the world wouldn't be broke and perplexed.

While most people spend most of their lives struggling to earn a living, a much smaller number seem to have everything going their way. Instead of just earning a living, the smaller group is busily working at building and enjoying a fortune. Everything just seems to work out for them. And here sits the much larger group wondering in awe how life can be so unfair, complicated, and unjust.

Dreams

So what's the major difference between the small group with so much and the larger group with so little? Despite all the factors that affect our lives—like our parents, the schools we attended, where we grew up—none has as much potential power for doing good as the ability to dream. Dreams are a projection of the kind of life we want to lead. Dreams can drive you. Dreams can make you skip over obstacles.

When we allow our dreams to pull us toward them, they unleash a creative force that can overpower everything in our way. To unleash this power, though, your dreams must be well-defined. A fuzzy future has little pull power. Well-defined dreams are not fuzzy. Wishes are fuzzy. To really achieve your dreams—to really have your future plans pull you—your dreams must be vivid.

If you've ever hiked a 14,000-foot peak in the Rocky Mountains, one thought has surely come to mind: How did the settlers of this country do it? How did they get from the East Coast to the West Coast by foot? Carrying one day's supply of food and water is hard enough. Can you imagine hauling all of your worldly goods with you mile after mile, day after day, month after month?

These people had dreams—big ones. They had ambition. They didn't focus on the hardship of getting up the mountain. In their minds, they were already on the other side; their bodies just hadn't gotten them there yet. Despite all of their pains and struggles, births and deaths, along the way, those who made it to the other side had a single vision—to reach the land of continuous sunshine and extraordinary wealth, to start over where anything was possible, where everything was possible. Their dreams were stronger than the obstacles in their way.

You have to be a dreamer. You have to see the future finished in advance. You have to seek California while you're climbing 14,000-foot peaks. You have to see the finish line while you're running the race. You have to hear the cheers when you're in the middle of a monster project. And you have to be willing to put yourself through the paces of doing the uncomfortable until it becomes comfortable—that's how you realize your dreams.

The United States was founded with dreams. They've always been important. Dreams are what caused thousands of people to leave their homes and families and start over in a land where anything was possible. To this day, dreams continue to bring people to our land of opportunity, to a country where you can start with little and end up with a lot.

Don't you sometimes wonder why so many immigrants who come to America can build a new life and a fortune while many of the people who were born here are barely surviving? The seekers have a dream, a defined goal, ambition. Aside from the pioneers who crossed the prairies and the mountains to reach their vision of hope and future promises, there are other amazing examples of how ambition has shaped the United States.

Seekers who succeed have a dream, goals, and ambition.

Take Ben Franklin, for instance. When most people think of Ben Franklin, they remember the kite and the lightning bolt and the discovery of electricity. What a lot of people may not know is that Ben Franklin was one of the first writers to address self-making. When Franklin started *Poor Richard's Almanack* in 1732, he used the blank spaces between the crop data and the weather information to insert clever bits of moral and practical advice. I'm sure you've heard the saying "Guests, like fish, begin to smell after three days." Well, that was one of hundreds of Ben Franklin's comments on life.

Another of his insights was "Diligence is the mother of good luck." It's amazing how hard-working, smart-working people have all the luck. We sometimes hear of a new musical group being an "overnight success." They must have been in the right place at the right time, knew the right people, had a friend to help them out. But in reality, their overnight success took several years. Another Franklin quote: "Energy and persistence conquer all things."

Success

I know that success is a relative term. It means different things to different people. To a school kid, success may mean a star on a difficult test. To a stay-at-home mother, it may mean a well-run household and a happy family. To an outside professional, it's most likely the thrill of closing a major contract, the pride in accepting a performance bonus or being named the top-producing salesperson. But the one thing heard from everyone who is successful is that they are happy with who they are and what they are doing. They are happy, content, satisfied. Success is a pleasure.

What have you done today that makes this day successful? Think about it and write it down. If at the end of the day, you can jot down the things that have made it a good day, you will soon see patterns forming. This is a good habit. When you can see a pattern of pleasure, you'll know you're on the road to success.

There are most probably people who have been working on a project for ten years and can think of themselves successful in their own right if they are honestly working toward it, doing everything to make themselves worthy of reaching the dream, really happy with where they are, doing it until then, maybe, they are a success. It's personal—going for it one step at a time, celebrating small accomplishments along the way for however long it takes.

Evidence of Change

So let's think about this for a moment. What outside evidence or results or proof do you see when you accomplish your goals one step at a time? Have you seen things change around you—little things, not major things, but minor, everyday things; things you may not even notice unless you are paying attention?

If you're one of those who would rather stay up late and get up late only to discover that your workplace doesn't fit your schedule, and you roll out of bed cursing the alarm clock every morning, maybe you could add a positive change by going to bed a half an hour earlier than normal. In time you may find out that you jump out of bed in a better mood, your day will start better, and you'll get more done. You may even notice that the people around you aren't so hard to work with after all.

Positive progress and change start by making one small change and adding to it every day. You can't change what's going on *around* you without first changing what's going on *within* you. Start changing how you look at mornings, and sure enough people will start changing how they look at you. When you start changing how you think, how you act, how you treat others, how you treat yourself and start responding, instead of reacting, to life, life will start responding in better and more positive ways to you.

You can make improvements in your lifestyle, sales career, business, relationships—with any part of your life—if you are willing to have a positive attitude and an unwavering work ethic. If you are looking for equities unmatched, don't curse the only thing you have—seed and soil, sunshine and rain, miracles and seasons—start processing your negatives into positives. You will be amazed at what will happen in a short period of time.

Positive progress and change start by making one small change.

So you ask yourself, "What small changes can I start making today that will be evident tomorrow?" Well, you can start in your car on your way to work. If you're sitting on the highway, stop-and-go traffic moving at about 15 miles per hour tops, look at the guy or the gal sitting in the car next to you and give them a smile or a thumbs-up or even wave. Some people might think you're a little strange, but hey, you'll feel better sharing a nice gesture.

And tomorrow when you get to work, how about a big cheery "Hello!" to everyone you see on the way to your workstation? And when you get home that night, how about giving your spouse and kids big hugs instead of collapsing on the sofa or your recliner?

When you start with the little things that make others happy and improve their day, the little things add up to big ones—for others and for yourself.

Take Charge

So what happens when you start taking charge of your own personal happiness, your own life? Do you think that these little things will somehow make a difference in meeting your goals? You bet they will. You can't do it alone. You can't be successful by yourself. It's hard to find a rich hermit.

The ambitious person realizes that each of us needs all of us. You, all by yourself, may have finalized the company's marketing plan, or finished the sales projections, or even written the mission statement for the year to come. Even if you did this all by yourself, you really had the help of all of those around you who tolerated and supported your need to be undisturbed or provided service to you during the project.

Maybe you should thank those people every once in a while with a dinner gift card, or flowers, or 18 holes of golf...even a thank-you note. Thank-yous are so important. After all, without your support team, you probably wouldn't be where you are today. You can't be successful by yourself. So thank them. Thank the people who assist you; let them know just how important they are to you, be it your office staff or your family or your friends. A thank-you goes a long way in showing your appreciation. So is it important to do a little extra for these people as you are working your way toward your goals? I think so. I'm sure you do too.

Set Sail

Once you've decided that you're going to set sail, go for it! Journey forth on your new charted course. Don't worry about the winds that will most certainly blow around you, the obstacles, the negativity that seem to stand in your way. Don't worry about what other people say. Just keep your mind on your course. The winds may blow fast and furious, but if you know your path, if you know where you are going, they will help push you toward the dreams and goals and treasures that you have already decided to go after.

Your goals will push you forward ahead of the stormy weather. There are some amazing people around to learn from today, people who have already braved the storms and came out on top. These are people who started with nothing and ended up with something great—famous people, not-so-famous people, maybe even people you know but don't know their stories; people who had an early vision and ambition; people who turned their focused dreams into the reality of success.

One of my friends tells this story about her dad. She thinks he's cheap because every time they go to an all-you-can-eat place, he eats all he can eat until he can't move, until he needs to take something for indigestion. But she knows where he came from, his history, and understands just why he is the way he is. He was raised in an orphanage, where he had to grab all he could or be hungry. But the real story behind her father is that he made himself a millionaire with nothing more than a dream. He watched his own father drown when he was four, was taken away from his mother a few years later and put into an orphanage because he was so bad. He was raised by other people, strangers.

After growing up in foster homes, my friend's father decided to go out on his own. He barely finished high school and then found a job as a vacuum cleaner salesman. He did well—really well. But the woman he loved didn't want to marry a vacuum cleaner salesman, and he really didn't want to be one, so he went to college, then went on to medical school. He prospered—really prospered. He led a tremendously successful life as a radiologist, then retired, goes fishing, rides his Harley. Stories of success are all around us, everywhere. Take the time to talk to successful people or read their stories. You most probably will learn some-thing—about them and yourself. You might find out that they have already traveled the path you are now on.

Ambition—a Moral Imperative

When most think of Jesse Jackson, we think of a political activist. But what most people don't realize is that before he went to the streets to gain votes, Jackson went to the ghettos with a message for inner-city youth. During his rallies, he would ask the street kids to repeat after him, "I am somebody." Jesse Jackson's message to these kids was that ambition is a moral imperative.

To be a good person, you have to have ambition. You have to try to do something good with your life. You have to try to get out of where you are today or make where you are a better place tomorrow. You have to. Anything else is a waste.

I'm sure you know that those same principles apply to you. When you get up tomorrow morning and are standing in front of the mirror getting ready for the day, remind yourself that you are somebody, you are important, and you can make the changes that will move you closer to realizing your ideal future.

Learn from other's secrets.

Reading about other people's success will motivate you, encourage you, and give you incentives to take action. Many people have written books about their life journeys that tell the stories and give the secrets we can all learn from.

Let's say you decide to take a trip—just a short one, maybe for a weekend—to a place you've never been before. Wouldn't you want to first ask someone who had already been there, "What's the best way to get there, the safest route, the quickest route? What do I need to bring to be totally prepared? What fun things should I look for on the way? What dangers do I need to avoid?" Talking with someone who has been there makes your trip that much more enjoyable.

It's the same thing with life. By listening to those who are further along in the journey—the journey you are interested in taking—and learning from their successes and failures, you will most probably pick up something that will make your journey that much better. Listening to the stories of others can be captivating, providing the extra push you've been looking for.

The successful ventures of others demonstrate what the power of ambition is truly all about. They've been there. Their knowledge is valuable. And when you use that knowledge and motivation to take action, you'll gain momentum to move forward with your plans.

Eventually you will find that the key to true motivation is right there inside you. You won't have to look elsewhere to get pumped up, turned on, charged up. With the right knowledge, you will learn how to motivate yourself. With the right knowledge, you will find yourself becoming inspired on your own by your own learning, by your own discovering.

You won't have to hope that somebody comes along to turn you on in the morning. They might not show up. You'll find that your journey of pursuit is the best alarm clock in the world.

The key to true motivation is right inside you.

So after we explore what ambition is and isn't, we will examine each of the six steps for igniting your ambition: self-direction, self-reliance, self-discipline, self-enterprise, working with others, and self-appreciation.

1

WHAT AMBITION IS AND ISN'T

Joseph Epstein wrote a book titled *Ambition* where he defines ambition as "the fuel of achievement."[1] He says that everybody has a need for achievement, to do well, to get somewhere in life, to be better, to achieve. Achievement means moving forward, and in order to move forward, you must be motivated, inspired, ambitious. You must have dreams and goals that create ambition—good ambition, positive ambition.

Ambition does not mean being greedy, selfish, or getting ahead at the expense of others. Ambition is not greed, an avarice, or an all-consuming desire for wealth. Ambition is not hoping you can win at the expense of others.

Do you suppose Judas—the Bible Judas who betrayed Jesus—was ambitious? He ended up with thirty pieces of silver, a fortune in those days. Was Judas successful because he had all that money? No, Judas sold out. Was Judas happy when it was all over with? No, the money didn't make him happy. What he did to get the money certainly didn't make him happy. What Judas became in the pursuit of his fortune caused him to end his own life. What drove him was not ambition; ambition is not greed.

Ambition is an eager desire to achieve; an eager desire to get ahead in life, to do more for your family, to prosper in health, wealth, and relationships.

Desire does not always translate into ambition. Desire is what you want for yourself. A bigger house, a better car, a fatter bank account, a better life—I desire to have these things. Ambition is how you get there. Desire is sometimes healthy and sometimes unhealthy. Desire might say, "I want the tallest building in town." The destructive side of desire might urge you to tear down all the other buildings. I guess that's one way to do it. You might get away with tearing down the first one and maybe the second one, but in your desire to tear them all down, sooner or later, some guy is going to be standing out in front of his building, saying, "I'm on to you. Get out of here." And pretty soon you're no longer known as a builder; you're known as a destroyer.

Ambition is creative, constructive, and an expression of yourself.

A second way to have the tallest building in town is to see it, dream it, plan it, put your team on it, work on it, go through all of the right steps to get there, and have the ambition to be the owner of the tallest building in town. If you really want it, have the skills to do it and the patience to weather all of the storms, your ambition will lead you there. Having the ambition to do what it takes to get you where you want to go is good. Ambition is creative and constructive. Ambition is an expression; it's something inside that you want to express in a positive way.

Dreams of Accomplishment

I'm sure you have dreams of accomplishing great things. Are you ambitious enough to realize your dreams? Are your dreams strong enough to pull you toward your future? Are they vivid enough to see the end result now? Are they worthy of doing until you get there?

What are your reasons for creating these dreams? I bet if you did a little soul searching, you could come up with a fairly strong list of reasons why it is so important to achieve your dreams. What are you trying to express? There are sometimes uniquely personal reasons. Some people do well for the recognition, some because of the way it makes them feel like a winner—and that is one of the best reasons. Once in a while, I hear someone say, "If I had a million dollars, I'd never work another day in my life." Hey, that's probably why the good Lord sees to it that the person doesn't get a million dollars. Family is another reason, a motivator for doing well. Some people do extremely well because of other people, and that's a powerful reason. Sometimes we will do something for someone else that we would not do for ourselves.

I know a lady who was getting back on track from financial disaster. Even though she didn't have much of anything left, her primary motivator was to keep her daughter in private school—an expensive one, one of the best in the country. Although her goal was to financially surpass where she was before her economic fall, her main reason to work all of those extra hours was to give her little girl the best possible education.

As you can well imagine, wanting to do something for someone else leads to all sorts of other accomplishments as well. How fortunate are the people who find themselves greatly affected by someone else? It's powerful.

Think about:

- What has you getting up early, hitting it hard all day and staying up late?

- What has you inspired?

- What are your reasons for doing well?

- What's at the core of your quest?

- What is the power behind your ambition?

Think some more about those questions, do some soul searching, define your reasons and jot them down so they will work for you.

Enlightened Self-Interest

So now we have determined that it's in your best self-interest and self-preservation to be ambitious. As human beings, we can't help but be interested in our own self-preservation; we can't help but be self-interested. It's one of the strongest urges we have—interested in our preservation, interested in our development, interested in our success. There's certainly nothing wrong with self-interest, but here's the bottom line: self-interest must be enlightened as to what truly serves us best.

When I found out that self-interest was okay, that was a big relief to me. I'm not talking about being selfish. Self-interest needs to be educated, enlightened. Self-interest is willing to be benefited by service to others, not at the expense of others. Self-interest at the expense of others can be greedy, evil, hoping you go up but someone goes down, hoping to attain while someone else loses.

27

"I win; you lose" is the beginning of awakening the dark side of our nature, wishing to benefit at the expense of others. That should not be.

Enlightened self-interest wishes to benefit at the service of others.

A friend of mine tells this story about a guy she heard from about every three months or so, soliciting money for food baskets for homeless families. She's happy to give her money to them. She was, unfortunately, homeless for a short period of time, and she knows the position these people are in. This group is legit; she checked them out. After this guy called several times, she started talking to him about other stuff. Turned out he was broke, living in a hotel, looking for any construction job he can find—any job at all. What was unique about this guy is that he donated two or three hours a night, every night from his hotel room, to call people and ask for donations to feed the homeless.

Most people would say, "This guy should use those hours every night to work a second job or a third job." But even though he's way down on the ladder of success, he believes it's important to help those less fortunate than he is. He has a roof over his head; he makes enough to feed himself. And my friend says that every time she talks to this guy every two or three months, he's doing better. He's digging himself out of debt, starting to save money, and he thinks he'll be able to move into an apartment in another month or two.

My friend was talking with an associate of hers who is single, lives in a big house, and needs to find a handyman to help her out on a regular basis, someone who can build an addition onto her house. So my friend told her about this guy. The only reason this guy was hired was because my friend's associate was touched by his dedication to service while he himself was down and out—success at the service of others. This guy isn't rich by any stretch, but through my friend's network, he now has constant work and is living in a place of his own. And guess what he does every night? He's still making phone calls to get money to feed the homeless. What great character this man has.

Enlightened self-interest leads to wealth. Self-preservation leads to poverty. Somebody says, "Well, I can't be concerned about other people. I have to pay attention to myself." Well, then you'll always have to. Somebody else says, "I can't be concerned about other people's bills. I have enough worries trying to pay my own." Well, then you'll have to worry about them for the rest of your life. The best way to get that monkey off your back is to turn your attention around. Once I understood that, I'm telling you, it revolutionized my whole life.

Self-interest is okay, but if you truly want to be happy, your self-interest must be enlightened, must be focused on others. It says, "Don't keep your attention on yourself if you want your life to work out well. Turn your attention to others and truly act in your own self-interest by making an investment in service to others."

Act in your own self-interest by making an investment in service to others.

Do More to Get More

My father taught me way back, "Son, always do more than what you get paid for." In my own self-interest, I did what my father taught me—to always do more than I got paid for. Why? To make an investment in my future, and it's paid off for me.

If you want that big promotion, are you going to go up to your boss and say, "Just give it to me. I'll work harder if you just give me that promotion"? No, it doesn't work that way. You have to do more in your current position so you get noticed, so you stand out from everybody else, so the boss says, "Hey, we have this position opening up, and I think we should give it to the person who routinely does much more than we expect." That would be you! You have to do more than you're paid for—it's an investment in your future.

I'm telling you, if you make a sale, you'll make a living. If you go beyond making the sale and serve people by keeping in touch, calling them before they call you, writing a thank-you note, sales will lead to multiple sales. You can make a fortune if you take care of your customers; they will open doors you can't get through by yourself.

Render fortunes of service.

All of us have found ways to make a living. What got interesting for me early on was to find ways to make a fortune. You may ask, "Well, how would I deserve to make a fortune?" It's easy. Render fortunes of service. People will do things for you that you won't believe if you routinely give them good service. One of the greatest gifts you can give anybody is the gift of attention. In return, they will do extraordinary things for your career, take you by the hand and lead you to more people than you could meet by yourself. Always do more than you get paid for.

Reap What You Sow

I believe life was designed to give us what we *deserve*—not necessarily what we *need*. When you understand that life principle, it's life-changing. The ancient law is *not* "If you need, you will reap." No, it doesn't work that way. A lot of people hope it works that way, but no, it doesn't. The ancient law is "If you plant, you will reap."

Somebody says, "Well, I really need to reap." Well, then you really need to have the ambition to plant. Your own self-interest needs to be educated in how to plant, how to do it so everybody wins, because life doesn't respond to need.

You can't go to the soil and say, "I need a crop." The soil just smiles at you and says, "Don't bring me your need; bring me some seed. Bring me some effort, some discipline, some ambition, some service. Bring me these things, and I'll return to you multiplied by two, five, ten times."

You can't come with need. You have to come with seed. You have to come with willingness, skills; willingness to learn, to change, to grow, to put yourself out, to stand up to the bad weather, to pull out the weeds, to nurture. That's the only way you get a return. Once you understand these principles, ambition truly becomes an exciting challenge, making sure everybody wins. Enlightened self-interest makes sure that everybody wins.

Education and Discipline

If you want to find, you must search—and if you search, you will find. To find what you are looking for, you must go to church, seminars, the library, bookstores, attend classes and training—you have to go searching. Why? When you search, you will find ideas, inspiration, hope, contacts, etc. Life reserves its treasures for those who deserve it, not those who need it.

Enlightened self-interest, or ambition, is giving to receive, searching to find, and ensuring everybody wins all the way around. Enlightened self-interest says, "I will learn that life is not just the passing of time. I will learn that life is the collection of experiences, ups and downs, highs and lows, laughter and tears." You must choose to act and have the discipline to follow through.

Now here's what's important about discipline—one discipline affects another discipline, and all disciplines affect each other. In fact, here's a good philosophical phrase: everything affects everything else. Nothing stands alone. Don't be naive and say, "This doesn't matter." Of course it matters. It all matters. Some things may matter more than others, but everything matters.

If you'd rather sleep in than go for a walk around the neighborhood, it will eventually matter to your health and wealth. If you'd rather spend your money instead of saving it, it will eventually matter when an emergency knocks on your door. If you'd rather put off writing a letter to an old friend, it will matter when the friendship fades away. If you'd rather work late every night instead of going home and spending time with your family, it will matter when they don't care if you come home at all. It all matters. Every letdown affects the rest.

If you won't even walk around the block for exercise, you probably won't eat right, and you probably won't buy the books you need to learn a trade, and you probably won't attend the seminars, and you probably won't spend your money wisely, and after years of this, it all adds up to an unproductive life. So the key to reversing this process is to be self-disciplined. It does matter; it all matters. (More about this important topic is coming up in Chapter 4.)

Life reserves its treasures for those who deserve it, not those who need it.

It All Matters

Now here's the positive side. Every new discipline affects the rest. Every new discipline makes a difference. That's why *action* is so important. The smallest action, the seemingly least important action, the action you think doesn't matter, does—it all matters.

Take this advice to heart, because when you start accomplishing and the value starts to return, you'll find inspiration to do the next action and the next one and the next one. If you start walking around the block, it'll inspire you to start eating healthy. Eating right will inspire you to read a book. Reading a book will inspire you to write your goals in a journal. Writing in a journal will inspire you to develop skills to reach your goals. Disciplines affect each other. Lack affects your life. The key is to diminish the lack and increase your resources.

One of our greatest temptations is to just ease up a bit, to do just a little bit less than we're capable of, to take a little break. You may think it won't make any difference, but it does. Not doing your best affects your consciousness, your attitude, your home life—everything. No, you can't ease up even a little bit. That's what vacations are for. When you're at work, work. When you're on vacation, rest. Wherever you are, be there.

If you think about vacation when you're at work, you'll surely think about work when you're on vacation. You'll just mess it all up, so be disciplined, get involved in the moment, do all that it takes to get the job done. Improve your health, get your bank account where it's supposed to be, build up your family relationships, get disciplined, be disciplined every day. When you set up the disciplines that give your life structure, miracles can happen—multiplied! And I'm telling you, anyone who wants to make a drastic change in their income can do it. I was broke at age 25 and a millionaire at age 31. Everything around me was the same—except me; I changed. I refined my philosophy, read the books, took classes, and started looking at life differently. I'm telling you, it works!

Six Principles to Build Ambition

The power of ambition discussed in this book rests on six principles that work together to create and direct energy toward achieving your goals in every aspect of your life. Each principle is thoroughly examined in separate chapters.

Specifically, the six principles that reveal the power of ambition are defined as:

1. **Self-direction:** Knowing who you are and where you want to go; accumulating the knowledge and being prepared for opportunities that come your way.

2. **Self-reliance:** Taking responsibility for your own life and for whatever happens to you; knowing that you have made the conscious decisions that are now affecting your life, that what's happening in your life is the direct result of your activity.

3. **Self-discipline:** Ambition at the daily level; knowing that you can reach your goals one step at a time, one day at a time, one activity at a time, and doing everything it takes to get there every day.

4. **Self-enterprise:** Consistently being able to create opportunity and consistently being able to take advantage of it; being aware enough to see it, skilled enough to make it work for you.

5. **Working with others:** We must make ourselves stronger to benefit all. We must succeed at the service of others, learning how to take our skills, enterprise, reliance, and direction to the table to create true success.

6. **Self-appreciation:** Appreciate your accomplishments; appreciate your potential, knowing that each day you complete all you set out to do, fueling your ambition by fueling your appreciation of yourself.

Each of these principles, when activated correctly, will develop your ambition, your eager desire to get more out of life, to gain wealth and prosperity, to enjoy family life, and to build a better business. All of these principles work together in creating and directing energy toward achievement and self-expression. All of these six principles are required to build the three cornerstones of a truly ambitious person: focused concentration, resilience, and integrity. You'll know you have unlocked the power of ambition when these three qualities become words that best describe you.

Note

1. Joseph Epstein, *Ambition: The Secret Passion*, 1980 (Chicago: Ivan R. Dee, 1989), 1.

2

PRINCIPLE 1: SELF-DIRECTION

As discussed in Chapter 1, ambition is the fuel of achievement, and that achievement is truly self-expression in its strongest and clearest form. So if achievement is based on self-expression, then it only makes sense that there is one true place to find ambition—inside yourself; in every thought, movement, and motivation.

Ambition is a result of positive self-direction.

Self-expression is really self-direction—how you think, how you move, how you motivate yourself. And ambition is a result of self-direction, which is one of the six principles for building ambition. Positive self-direction says, "I know who I am, and I know where I want to go. I am accumulating knowledge, and experiences, and feelings, and philosophies that prepare me for opportunities that I know will show up without notice."

Positive Self-Direction

You know who you are and where you want to go. You've already spent a great deal of time thinking about it. You've been working on the parts of your personality that will make you better; working on your attitude, working on your health, working on your time management skills, putting it all down on paper, and you constantly see yourself in the place where you want to be.

As you talk with yourself every day, how often do you ask:

- Is what I'm doing today getting me closer to where I want to be tomorrow?

- Am I making the daily adjustments necessary?

- Am I doing all that it takes?

- Will I keep on doing it until direction determines destination?

- Are all of the disciplines I'm currently engaged in taking me where I want to go?

- Are all of the disciplines I am presently engaged in taking me where I want to go?

What important questions to ask at the beginning of the month, the week, at the beginning of the day—because here's what you don't want to ever do: kid yourself. Kid your neighbor and kid me and kid the marketplace, if you want to, but gosh, you can't kid yourself. You can't kid yourself by crossing your fingers and hoping you'll arrive at a good destination when you're not even headed that way. You think maybe the wind will take you in the right direction? Well, there's a chance yes—and no.

You have to take charge. You have to ask yourself often, "Am I...?" "Am I disciplining myself in the direction I want to go?" Don't be faked out thinking you are on the way to financial success when there's not a prayer, not a hope. Don't be faked out hoping there's someone who will take care of it, take care of me.

They aren't going to take care of it. They aren't going to take care of you. That responsibility is yours.

What if all of your negatives turned positive? What would that do for your fortune and your future? Not much. If prices come down a little, what would that do for your fortune, and your future, and your sophistication, and your culture? Not much. If the economy gets a little better? Not much. If you don't make plans of your own, you'll fit into someone else's plans. And guess what they have planned for you? You're right—not much.

Most people wake up every morning counting on this "not much" list. And that's why what they have is not much hope, not much promise, not much progress. They're driving what they don't want to drive, living where they don't want to live, doing what they don't want to do. Forget the thief waiting in the alley to snatch your wallet; what about the thief in your mind? Many are lazy, not stimulated by thoughts and questions.

Don't become a victim of yourself.

To keep from becoming a victim of yourself, ask yourself these questions:

- Is this the direction I want for my life?

- Is it someone else's direction for my life?

- Is this a goal I have been ingrained with since my childhood?

- Is it my parents', or my spouse's, or my boss's, or my children's goal?

- Is it mine?

Ask yourself—debate with yourself—these questions. Debate the ideas I am sharing with you in this book. After you've heard all the ideas, debate what will work for you and won't work for you.

But most importantly, get into the debate of your inner mind and ask, "What am I doing that works? What am I doing that doesn't work?" Debate it all. Work within your mind to figure out the best possible direction for *you*. Determine your self-direction.

You hear stories all the time of middle-class and upper-middle-class kids having problems. Their parents are highly successful; they want their kids to be highly successful, but the kids are having problems—maybe not with their grades, but with how they feel about themselves. Sometimes parents push their kids in one direction, perhaps to take over the family business or follow in the family career footsteps. It's the parents' direction, not the kids' direction. The kids know that something's just not right, and that leads to problems.

Lessons Learned

I know a woman who comes from a "medical family"; everyone has some type of career in medicine. All the kids grew up and became a doctor. Now, it wasn't a bad upbringing; they had everything they needed, but they also had the extra push to go into medicine. As a matter of fact, my friend says that they were raised with such tunnel vision that she didn't even have the slightest idea how food got into the grocery store, how cars got into the lots, how money got into the banks. She didn't know. The issues were never brought up at the dinner table.

She remembers the first time she looked for a job to make extra money while attending college. The best jobs listed in the newspaper, the ones for qualified people, were advertising a monthly salary of $900. She thought the average person on the street, the average non-qualified person, made at least $3,000 a month. What a difference, what a shock, to be so sheltered from real life, to be so far off in what the average person made for a living. It was a real revelation for her.

So she started asking questions. If she was that far off in her judgment of average earnings, maybe she was way off on other thoughts in life too. Maybe there was more to life than being in medicine. Maybe this wasn't what she wanted to do after all. Maybe she finally found the reason why she hadn't been happy through all of her academic achievements. Sure enough, she figured out that the medical goals were not her own, only those of her parents.

And even though she was chastised by her family for not following through with the family goals, she is now much happier following her own path. *Direction must be your own, or it can eventually damage your soul, spirit, and even your health.*

There's another important part to my friend's story of growing up that her family doesn't talk about, yet it happened. While my friend was pushing for perfection in school, she also pushed herself into an eating disorder, anorexia. A few years later, about the same time she started asking questions about life, she determined, with the help of a specialist, that this eating disorder had nothing to do with food, or the lack of it. It had to do with control. It had to do with somebody else's direction for her.

Direction has to be your own or it can be damaging. Parent, be watchful how you motivate your children. Give them all of the resources to make their own choices, and back them up. Give them the freedom to discover their own direction. It may not be the direction you'd hope for, but it is their direction. And with their own direction, they will reach their own destination. It just doesn't work out any other way.

Your Own Direction in Life

If you are one of those people who had the revelation that the life and goals you're pursuing are not your own, you can change it, just like my friend did. Change doesn't come overnight, but the direction of life can come overnight. A new goal can reach out and grab you in one day, give you the push and the ambition and the momentum to change your course. You can determine where you want to be, but the final destination does not happen overnight. It takes time and a lot of work for the plans to build, to grow, to run the course. Reaching your goals takes patience.

Let's say you have a brilliant idea for starting a new company; what's the first thing you do? You write a business plan, and a marketing plan, and complete the financial pro formas. You don't expect to have an idea one day and a prospering business the next. No, it doesn't work that way. You have to take all the right steps, give it care and nurturing and time—lots of time for your investment to start reaping rewards. You have to be patient.

45

But here's what does happen: As soon as you turn toward a new direction, you have an excellent chance of a brand-new destination in a few years—not a brand-new destination tomorrow. You will reach your own personal destination as surely as you follow and adhere to the disciplines required.

Two Parts to Positive Self-Direction

There are two parts to positive self-direction: *self-knowledge* and *self-preparation*.

Self-Knowledge

Self-knowledge is knowing who you are and what you want to do with your life. Self-knowledge is knowing how you feel about yourself. Self-knowledge has a lot to do with your philosophy, and your philosophy has a lot to do with shaping your attitude—how you feel about yourself, how you feel about life, how you feel about your direction, how you feel about others around you, your attitude.

You have to gather enough knowledge and information to know what's right for you. How do you gather up information? Start with your own experiences. The best way to know if something works for you the right way is to do it the wrong way. Don't keep doing it the wrong way; you have to be smart enough to think, *Hey, this isn't working, so I'm going change it.* Then search for the knowledge and apply what's right for you in your life.

Develop your own attitudes and philosophies around your own experiences and the experiences of others. Take all the information you have gathered and compile it, consider it, debate it, tear it apart, turn it upside down. Look at it from your own perspective and refine it to suit you, rearrange it, throw some of it out. Keep what you think will work for you.

And most importantly, make sure that what you end up doing is the product of your own conclusion. Make sure that the knowledge you are building is your own self-knowledge. The first component of positive self-direction is self-knowledge.

Self-Preparation

The second component of positive self-direction is self-preparation. Self-preparation means being ready for the opportunities when they show up in your life. Being ready for the sales call that may make you a fortune. Being ready for the meeting that may positively affect your career. Being ready in expectation that opportunities will come.

If you are a parent, when you found out that a new member of the family was going to come along in nine months or so, what did you do? You started getting ready—you prepared for the arrival of the baby. You read about how to best handle a baby. You bought everything needed to care for the baby. You asked questions of friends and relatives who already have a baby or two. As best as possible, you defined your parenting style and prepared for the major change coming in how you live, the changes in waking/sleeping hours, and the financial obligations you have to live up to. You prepared.

Well, preparing for your own life is pretty much the same: defining a goal, planning a goal, knowing that with enough planning and dedication and hard work, you will meet your goal. You know that it will be tough for the first few years, but the sacrifice is well worth it. So in the meantime, you have to be ready for it.

If you wish to be ruler over many, you have to be faithful with few. If you wish to have power and influence over many, be the leader of many and get the return from many, be faithful when there's just a few—"faithful" meaning "disciplined" when there are just a few, which prepares you for the many to come. Being disciplined in your own enlightened self-interest gives you the best chance to be the ruler, or have power, influence, or a place of honor among the many. Be faithful when there are just a few.

Some may say, "If I had a big organization, I'd really pour it on. I'd manage it with competence and expertise. But I only have a few, so I don't know how to begin." Come on, that's not logical. When you have just a few, you can begin where you are with the same competence and expertise you claim you have. If you have a few employees, a few distributors, a few salespeople, that's the time to sharpen your communication skills, get prepared for more, and give the most of your heart and soul to build your business. In your own enlightened self-interest, set up lines of communication when there's a few so it's in place when there are many. Be totally absorbed when there's just a few so you can spread yourself when there are many. If working for someone else, put yourself in line for promotion by earning an excellent reputation with skills and dependability so when a leadership position opens with the many, you'll be called.

Being prepared is the key.

The same key applies to your money. Some may say, "Oh, if I had a fortune, I'd really take good care of it, but I only have a paycheck and I don't know where the money goes."

Wow, did you ever hear or say something like that? Positive self-direction knows that close attention to handling just a few dollars will lead to managing larger dollar amounts. Positive self-interest, positive self-direction, positive self-preparation welcomes tomorrow by doing all that you can today toward reaching your goals.

Set Your Goal

What a brand-new reason for setting goals, what an all-encompassing challenge to have a better vision of the future, to see what it will make of you to achieve it. And here's why: *the greatest value in life is not what you get; it is what you become.* The major question to ask on the job is not "What am I *getting* here?" The most vital question to ask is "What am I *becoming* here?"

It's not what you get that makes you valuable; it's what you *become* that makes you valuable. Set the kind of goals that will make something of you to achieve them.

So there you have the two components of positive self-direction: self-knowledge, knowing who you are and what you want to do with your life; and self-preparation, getting ready for the opportunities before they come your way.

You need both aspects for positive self-direction: figuring out who you are and what you want and being prepared for the day you reach your goals—being ready, being worthy, becoming the person you need to be in pursuit of what you want. What good is an opportunity if you're not prepared to take advantage of it? It's no good.

Set a goal that makes you stretch for what it will make of you to achieve it.

Self-Knowledge Acid Test

Now here's what's called the self-knowledge acid test. Without thinking too much about it, quickly list your three most important long-term, work-related goals. Is it a client you've been trying to sign for several months? Is it a major sale you've been trying to make? Is it a promotion? Is it a partnership in the firm?

_____
_____
_____
_____
_____
_____
_____

Again, without thinking too much about it, quickly list your three most important personal and spiritual goals—things that will make a difference in your personal life. Is it going to church more often than holidays, grasping all you can from the Sunday sermon? Is it spending more quality time with your kids? Is it turning the TV off during the dinner hour and actually talking about the important things in life with your family? Is it making more dates with your spouse? Is it planning a much-needed family vacation? Is one of them making a conscious effort to exercise more, to eat better, to lose some weight, to get in shape? What are the three most important personal and spiritual goals you have? *Quickly* write them down. Doesn't matter what they are, just write them down.

Now, take some time to really visualize what the achievement of these goals would look like. What does your future hold for you if you landed that big client? What does your future look like if you got that promotion, if you spent more time with your family, if you planned more outings with your spouse? What does your future look like?

Really spend some time on this important acid test. Ask yourself, *Is this really my goal? Is this truly what I want? Is it a positive goal? Is it important enough to me to become what it takes to reach this goal? Is it mine? Is it worth it?* If your three goals on the career side and three goals on the personal side don't stand up to these questions, take time to carefully redefine your list. Redefine where these goals came from. Redefine what is actually important to you. Redefine how hard you'll really work to get them.

Two Goal-Setting and Redefining Processes

There are two parts to the goal-setting and redefining process: don't set your goals too low and don't compromise. Let's look at each more closely.

Number one: Don't set your goals too low.

An interesting thing we teach in leadership: don't join an easy crowd; you won't grow. Go where the expectations are high. Go where the demands are high. Go where the pressure is on to perform, grow, change, develop, read, study, and develop skills.

Number two: Don't compromise. Don't sell out.

There were some things I went for back in those early years that I paid too big a price for. If I'd known back then how much it was going to cost me, I never would have gone for them, but I didn't know. Don't sell out. An ancient phrase says, "Count the costs." Count the cost: if it won't make you happy to get it, if you become less in your pursuit of getting it, if it's not worth the life you'll lead after you get it, it's not worth it.

Now let's talk a little more about self-preparation. Self-preparation has two benefits: (1) it moves you toward your goal, and (2) it refuels your ambition—your activity refuels your ambition. You already have your goal in mind, you know where you want to go, you're getting ready for it, you're doing all the things you're supposed to do, and by getting ready to achieve your goals, you're moving closer to your goals. That's how it works.

The second major benefit to self-preparation is that it refuels your ambition; your activity refuels your ambition. The things that you are doing today are getting you ready for tomorrow. It's exciting! You know that you're getting closer every day. Ambition must be kept alive, be kept active, must continue to move forward; otherwise, you're just daydreaming. You must keep active, keep moving forward, so your ambition can fuel you, motivate you, get you where you want to be.

This method of self-preparation involves three steps:

1. Consider your resources.

2. Determine what you have to do to get ready.

3. Expedite the opportunities.

Let's examine these steps individually.

Step one:

Carefully consider where the next opportunity for reaching your goal will originate. Where will it come from? Will it come from networking with your colleagues? Will it come from reading the last book you bought—the book that's still sitting on your shelf, waiting to give you some answers? Will it come from you taking the time to think it out? Where will it come from?

53

If you don't know where the next opportunity will come from that will push you forward, here's a suggestion: For each of your major goals, the top priorities on your list, take out a separate piece of paper—one single sheet per major goal—and write down your goal at the top of each sheet. Then list all reasonable resources. Write down every possible place that you could find the opportunity to achieve this goal. Then classify each resource, asking yourself, *Is this resource a sure thing, a good bet, about even chances, unlikely, a long shot?* Ask yourself these questions, and classify all of the resources you have written down. That's the first step.

Step two:

Make sure you know what you need to do to be prepared for your opportunities. Take your sure things first. Figure out what you need to do to be prepared when an opportunity presents itself. Break down your preparation into concrete steps so you know exactly what you have to do to take advantage of the opportunity when it comes your way.

Let's say that one of the top priorities on your career list of goals is to get a specific new client. Let's take it one step further to say that on your resource list for this goal is to have a lunch meeting with a friend who just happens to be the mentor of the client you're going after. Is this friend of yours a sure bet on your resource list? Let's say he is. You know this guy is a tremendous consulting source for the client you want and listens to the opinions and advice of your friend. When getting ready to have lunch with your friend, make sure you're up to date about the industry data that will impress your friend, making him realize someone he knows could benefit from your knowledge, and your vitality, and your spirit, and your experience. Impress him so much that he goes to his friend, the client you're after, and tells this prospective client of yours that he needs to do business with you. That's being prepared!

Go through each goal sheet with your list of resources and classify each one. Break each resource into concrete steps of preparation. Start by working on the sure bets first, and then move down the line. The long shots will come through every so often, but start with the resources that will serve you best now. Get ready for the opportunities before they come your way.

Step three:

Expedite the opportunities. What can you do to increase the likelihood of this opportunity and make it happen as quickly as possible? Go over it and over it and over it. Look at all the angles. Use these three methods again and again as you assess where you are now and where you have to go next to keep moving toward the achievements that are most important to you.

This method of self-preparation works wherever you are in your journey, whether you're close to your goals or just starting your journey of self-direction. This method works. Have working knowledge to draw from. Continually work on yourself in preparation for where you want to be. Build a reservoir of thoughts, and ideas, and philosophies, and experiences that are your own. Build, grow, change, get ready, be prepared for a life worth living.

Four *Ifs* of a Worthwhile Life

The following are four *ifs* that make life worthwhile:

1. *Life is worthwhile* ***if*** *you learn.* There is nothing worse than being stupid. Learn from your personal experiences. Learn from other people's experiences. Read. Take classes. Interview people. Seek a mentor. There are many amazing things to learn about business trends, family relationships, nature, sports, medicine, economics—the list is endless. Strive to keep learning through-out your life.

2. *Life is worthwhile* ***if*** *you try.* Now you have to take what you've learned and see if you can try your hand at it. Someone may say, "Well, you can't *try*; you have to *do*." No, you have to try. For example, I put the bar up two feet and ask the kids, "Who can jump two feet?" "I can," some say. "I can't," some say. "I don't know," some say. How will they find out what answer is true? They don't until they try. What if you try your hand at something and it doesn't work? You try again a different way. You keep trying until it works. When the record book on you is finished, let it show your wins and your losses, not that you didn't even try.

3. *Life is worthwhile* ***if*** *you stay.* You have to learn to stay committed to reaching your goal. You don't have to stay forever, just stay till you see it through. Don't be the person who builds a foundation, then wanders off somewhere and builds another foundation. There are foundations scattered across the country but no walls, no roofs—just a bunch of foundations. This is not the way to build a good reputation. Stay until it is finished.

4. *Life is worthwhile* ***if*** *you care.* Caring is a unique, vital, and powerful human experience that is far reaching. If you care at all, you'll see results. If you care enough, you can get magnificent results.

To lead a life worth living, you have to learn, try, stay, and care. Develop your positive self-direction. Do what we've discussed in these first few chapters and you're on your way to building a life worth living through the power of ambition.

3

PRINCIPLE 2: SELF-RELIANCE

The second principle of building ambition is self-reliance, which includes:

- Taking responsibility for your own life

- Taking responsibility for whatever happens to you

- Knowing you have consciously made the decisions that are now affecting you

- Knowing that what is happening now today is the direct result of your activity, what you did yesterday

- Counting on yourself

- Trusting yourself

- Being confident with yourself

- Being responsible to yourself

- Trusting your own instincts

- Trusting the conclusions you have developed from your study of experiences and philosophies

- Taking the credit that is due you

- Learning from the mistakes you have made

By being prepared, you increase your chances of success, your likelihood of seizing opportunities when they come your way, of being ready within yourself to take advantage of once-in-a-lifetime situations. Some people tend to blame others for their mistakes and failures. Kelly may say, "It's not my fault the report isn't done. John didn't do his part." Of course it's Kelly's fault too; it was a joint-effort report. Taking responsibility is the right thing to do.

Considering this scenario, as an employee, you can't totally control what others around you do, but it's in your own best self-interest to stay on top of things, especially if it's going to affect your future. Do you think your boss cares that John didn't do his part? Do you think he sees John as the bad guy? Of course not. All the boss sees is that the report isn't done—bottom line.

Be responsible for what affects you. Check in with people who are working with you, the people who make up your team. You can be more responsible by saying, "Hey, John, how are you doing with your part? Do you need some help? Can we put somebody else in here to help you finish?"

If you are a manager and John consistently doesn't handle his part, you have to replace him. If he isn't doing his share, you have to find somebody who will. Or what? It will negatively affect you. You can't wake up the morning the project is due hoping and wishing that John has done his part. No, you have to be responsible, because his laziness will affect your career.

Very early on in my career, my approach to a better future was to just go through the day with my fingers crossed. I used to say something like, "I sure hope things will change for the better." Then I found out that nothing would change until I changed. When I change for the better, my future changes for the better. If you change, it'll all change. Don't put it on someone else or hope that someone else will change your future for you. Take responsibility for yourself. Take personal responsibility. Be self-reliant, while keeping others in mind.

Change What You Can

You can't change the seasons or the wind, but you can change your habits. You can change what you have charge over. You can change your behavior from watching television every night to attending night school. You can go to a sports game on the weekends or you can learn new skills needed to reach your goals. You have control over those types of circumstances. If you don't, it's your fault. You have to take personal responsibility and be self-reliant. You, you, you. Nobody else can change your life, alter your ambitions, pave a golden road for you—only you can. It's up to you. Be responsible for yourself.

Learn to reap the harvest without complaint. This is a sign of growing maturity, which comes from taking full responsibility for yourself, for everything you do. Be responsible for and to yourself. It's your crop to harvest. Whatever your paycheck is, take full responsibility. You say, "Well, it's my employer." No, it's not your employer. You can become twice as valuable, three times as valuable, by burning the midnight oil, learning more skills, and bringing more value to the marketplace. I'm telling you, whatever your harvest is, take it without complaint. Take it without blaming others.

Self-preparation leads to control over your life. As discussed in the previous chapter, whenever you prepare correctly, take all the necessary steps, do everything in your power to stay on track, your preparations will lead to success and you will achieve your goals. Success leads to reinforcement of the proper disciplines.

Positive Reinforcement

If what you're doing is working, keep doing it. If what you're doing isn't working, change it. When you are doing all that you can possibly do and are successful at reaching your expectations, keep doing it. Successes are positive reinforcement for future successes. With positive reinforcement, we train our dogs and teach our kids. With positive reinforcement, the trainers at Sea-World can get a killer whale to do tricks and follow commands and work side by side with humans.

When you bring a puppy home and train him not to mess in the house, you reward him for going outside or scratching at the door. When potty training your toddler, you reward the youngster with accolades and/or a snack for learning something new. When instructing your kids to do their homework and study, you reward them when they get good grades. You teach them that the skills they are developing now will have great positive effects on their lives later, but you reward them now. This is positive reinforcement. The greater the value, the greater the reward. The better you do, the better your reward. For you, the greater the value, the greater the reward, such as a bigger paycheck, a better house, financial freedom—it's all a reward system.

There are two major benefits of positive reinforcement: positive reinforcement (1) builds good habits and (2) creates the energy to fuel additional achievement.

If the habits you have are building your ambition and increasing your success, keep doing them. Your success reaffirms these habits are good.

On the other side, when reviewing your habits, you may find that some are actually inhibiting your success. You may find that what you're doing every day is bad for you. You may realize that you don't have very good habits and that you need to make changes.

Someone may say, "Well, I got out of the habit of taking my daily walk around the block." Well, I guess you'll just have to get in the habit of being sick down the road. Or, "Well, I used to read books all the time. I just got out of the habit." Then I say, get back into the habit. Go back to your disciplines that bring success.

You can keep your fingers crossed and hope that your career, family life, and/or health will all straighten out. You can wish for the wind not to blow quite as severely, to change in your favor, but that way of thinking and living is naive at best. If your habits aren't serving you, change them. Don't wish for a better wind—take steps to gain the wisdom to set a better sail. Utilize whatever wind that blows to take you where you want to go. That is the philosophy I picked up at age 25, and it revolutionized my whole life.

Easy Does It

Here's what I found: I found that making changes was easy. I became a millionaire when I was 31, and I found it was easy. Here's my definition of easy: doing something you can do. I figure if it's something I can do, it's easy. But here is the caveat: I worked hard at it. I made sure my disciplines were in line. I made sure my habits were good. I made sure I did all that I could.

I found something that I could do, and then I worked hard at it. I got up early, stayed up late, and worked hard—from ages 25 to 31. But what I did was easy for me, meaning it was something I could do. "Well," you say, "Mr. Rohn, if it was so easy, how come during those six years all those other people around you didn't get rich?"

Here's why.

It's easy to keep doing what doesn't work. It's easy to keep bad habits. It's easy *not* to develop the disciplines. Why did I get rich and they didn't? Here's a philosophical phrase to answer that question: *the things that are easy to do are also easy not to do.* That's the difference between success and failure, between day-dreams and ambitions.

The key formula for success—a few well-thought-out disciplines practiced every day.

Here is the key formula for success: a few well-thought-out disciplines practiced every day. What should you spend your time doing? Don't waste your time on things that aren't going to matter. But a few simple disciplines can change your whole economic future, your family's future, the future of your business, enterprise, sales career, management career—your entire life. A few simple disciplines, a few simple habits, good habits repeated every day is the key to the life you envision.

Now here's the formula for failure: repeatedly making judgment errors every day. All you have to do is make a few errors in judgment and repeat them every day, and your life will spin out of control in ten years. You could end up driving what you don't want to drive, wearing what you don't want to wear, living where you don't want to live, and earning what you don't want to earn. A few errors every day, along with bad habits, lead to disaster.

It's easy to repeat an error in judgment because failure doesn't fall at the end of the first day. Bad habits don't show their horrible results at the end of the first day, the first week, or the first month. It's easy to get fooled. If disaster fell on us at the end of the first week, we'd change our philosophy. But the results of judgment errors and bad habits are so subtle that they move you off course little by little. You keep drifting off course until eventually you're totally adrift.

You have the choice right now of one of two "easys"—easy to do or easy not to do. I can give you in one sentence how I got rich by the time I was 31. For six years, I did not neglect to do the easy things I could do. *I did not neglect* is the key. I found something easy I could do that led to fortune, and I did not neglect to do it.

The major reason for anyone not having more of what they want when living in the United States—more health, more money, more power, more influence, more everything—is simple neglect. If you don't take care of neglect, it becomes an infection, and then it becomes a disease. If you're in the habit of not doing all it takes to get ahead, get in the habit of doing it. Doing all it takes is the first benefit of positive reinforcement—building good habits.

Creating Energy for Achievement

The second benefit of positive reinforcement is that it creates the energy to fuel additional achievement. It gives you the drive to do more—to not only keep on doing what's right, but to do more of what's right…the disciplines that help you grow and get ahead of it all. The knowledge that what you're doing is paying off creates more energy to keep going.

How easy is it to get up in the morning when you know you're not doing all that it takes? It's not very easy at all. You can just lay there awake, thinking, *Oh, what's a few more minutes in bed? It won't matter much anyway.* Wrong. It does matter. It will matter.

Now, how easy is it to get up in the morning when you're pouring it on, doing the best you can, anxious to get going, making progress toward your dreams? It's a whole different story.

Resting to renew your reserves is much different from resting to avoid your day. When you're psyched up and excited for what you've planned to accomplish for the day, it's amazing—you'll wake up before the alarm clock even tries to startle you awake. Your successes fuel your ambition. Your successes give you extra energy. Your successes pave the way for more successes. It's the snowball effect. With one success, you're excited to meet another and another and another. Soon, the disciplines that were so difficult in the beginning, the disciplines that got you going, are now part of your philosophy.

How do you know when you're successful? Do you have to be a millionaire? No. But you should earn all you possibly can. If you earn $10,000 a year and that's the best you can do, that's enough. God and everything else will see to it that you're okay. The key is to just do the best you can. If it's $10,000 a year, wonderful. If it's $100,000 a year, wonderful. If it's $1 million a year, wonderful. It doesn't matter the dollar amount as long as you've done the best you possibly can. Earn and be the most you possibly can. Here's why: the essence of life is growth—to do the best you can.

The essence of life is growth.

Here's what's interesting: humans are the only life form that will do less than they possibly can and will settle for less. Other life forms strive for maximum capacity. For example, how tall will a tree grow? As tall as it possibly can. Trees send their roots down as deep as possible, stretch their limbs up as high as possible, produce every leaf and every fruit possible. As a matter of fact, a human keeps growing physically until we're done. That's part of life we can't control, because it's genetically coded. That's probably why we keep growing until we're done—because we can't control that part.

It's the rest of our growing that we control—the growing and expansion of our minds, which tends to get away from us. Why wouldn't human beings strive for their maximum possibility? Here's why: because we've been given the dignity of choice. It makes us different from alligators and trees and birds. The dignity of choice makes us different from all other lifeforms.

Here are our choices:

1. To become *part* of what we could be

2. To become *enough* to get by

3. To become *all* we can be

My best advice for you is to choose No. 3—the *all*. Earn all you can. Make all the friends you can. Read as many books as you can. Develop as many skills as you can. See as much as possible. Do as much as possible. Make as much fortune as possible. Give as much of it away as possible.

Live to the max; there's no life like it. I'm telling you, once I got on track, I've never looked back.

Pick up the challenge. Go for it. Take the best of the two easys. Take the self-reliance route that says it's easy to get ahead, it's easy to do all you can, it's easy to succeed, it's easy to have financial freedom. The more you do, the more you get.

The two primary benefits of positive reinforcement are to build good habits and to create more energy to fuel your ambitions, your desires, and your achievements.

Write About It

How can you isolate what's working for you and what isn't? How can you make sure that you are reinforcing your positive disciplines? Well, if it isn't apparent and easy to see right away, if what you're doing is happening in such small increments that you're not sure you're on track, then you need to write it down. At the least, keep a journal.

If you really aren't sure that what you're doing is making measurable progress, you need to keep a written record. You need to write down everything that may be relevant in your day: what you did, who you saw, what you felt, how it may or may not affect you now and in the future. The best way to track your activities of the day is to write them down. The best way to track your activities of the week is to write them down. The best way to analyze your progress throughout the year is to have written it down. Why? So you can review it and compare. And it makes you more accountable to yourself. By putting into writing the action steps that you have planned, you will easily see what works and what doesn't.

Gifted people choose to learn from each day.

Most people just try to get through the day, never writing anything down, never keeping track of their progress along the way, never really knowing if they are doing all they can to reach their goals, to drive their ambition. But gifted people choose to learn from each day. They don't let a day end without noting a valuable experience, emotional content, an idea that may positively affect their future.

To get the most and learn the most from every day, you need to reflect on each day. How can you reflect on a day unless you record it in history? How can you possibly reflect on a week or a month or a year unless you can look back and analyze it? How can you learn from past mistakes and bask in past successes unless you write it all down?

There's something mysterious about writing out a problem. It's almost as though when you start writing, you start figuring out ways to make it work. Perhaps the act of writing makes you see it objectively. You can start to see where you fit into the picture—if you are being responsible and self-reliant. You are pondering while writing, trying to figure it all out. The fact that it is now on paper (or computer/phone screen) actually creates a space between you and the problem. In this space that you have created, solutions now have room to grow. Writing about occurrences helps you understand exactly what is happening and/or has happened.

When we describe life to ourselves only in our minds, our imaginations tend to feed back to us false or distorted information. Sometimes our creativity can create scenarios that really don't exist at all if we keep the information solely in our mind. But by writing it all down, we can become more factual, more accurate, more realistic, more logical. Then as we reread what we have written, we create a new picture in our mind. When we see things as they are rather than how we think they are, we can make them better.

It's all part of being responsible. It's all part of seeing things objectively to fully understand the steps we must take to make things better, the steps we must take to better prepare ourselves for the opportunities that lie ahead.

The Best Cheerleader—You

Now let's turn to those times when you thought you were pre-pared, prepared, prepared—yet things just didn't work out. Let's take a few minutes to talk about the importance of knowing your-self enough to be your best cheerleader. You know, the times you need a cheerleader when you thought you were doing what you were supposed to do and were misinformed; the times you thought you had it all laid out, and it just didn't work; the times when you burned the midnight oil day after day, and it didn't seem to help—it didn't seem to change the end result—these are the times that you have to rely on your own self-encouragement.

There are two ways to use self-encouragement: (1) take respon-sibility for the missed opportunity or the misrepresentation and (2) remind yourself that you're bound to improve.

Learn from the fact that even though your client wanted it one way and you presented it the right way, it didn't work. Be prepared for the letdowns that happen every so often. Know that this lost opportunity just sets you up better to win the next opportunity. Realize that you can make the necessary alterations next time, make the changes that will make the difference. Study your mistakes and learn from them. Don't dwell on the mistakes. Acknowledge them; learn from them. Encourage yourself that you're smarter than your bank account leads you to believe.

The second way to use self-encouragement is to remind your-self that you're bound to improve. Don't get down on yourself. Don't beat yourself up. It's the next opportunity that matters—not the last one, the *next* one. The last one matters only in that you must learn from your mistakes, but the next one gives you the opportunity to show what you learned from your mistakes. You can do it better next time. You just have to practice, practice, practice.

Don't beat yourself up for messing up; pat yourself on the back for figuring it out.

Keep trying—keep trying until you have it down to a science. If you figured out what went wrong last time, you now know how to make it right next time. If you figured out what was in your presentation that didn't work, delete it. If you didn't close the deal last time because you didn't have all the facts and figures in place, determine to have all the facts and figures in place next time. Don't beat yourself up for messing up; pat yourself on the back for figuring it out.

You need to encourage yourself, pump yourself up, and be your own cheerleader. Why? Because you can't wait and hope that someone else will come along and cheer you up, make you feel better, tell you that you'll do better next time. You have to rely on yourself—be self-reliant. You must have faith in yourself and your ability to figure out what works and what doesn't, what's right and what's wrong. You must have the inner belief that everything you're doing is for a positive outcome in the future. You must encourage yourself with future successes. Encourage yourself by believing in your goals, your dreams, your ambition. Know that you have a plan, you're taking the right steps, and you're going to stay with it until everything works out.

When you miss an opportunity, are unprepared for an opportunity, or suffer a setback while reaching for your goals—when you miss out—you need to encourage yourself by immediately getting back into line. There's an old cowboy saying: "Fall off a horse seven times and you're a real cowboy." Likewise, if you fall off track, get right back on. If you fall out of a good habit, jump right back in. If you fall away from your disciplines, get back to them as quickly as possible. If you fall off the horse—the horse of habits, disciplines, or progress—climb right back in the saddle. It may be hard or a bit frightening, but get back on. Keep your ambition alive and active and well.

Discipline weighs ounces; regret weighs tons.

We all suffer from one of two pains—the pain of discipline or the pain of regret. If you don't suffer an ounce of discipline, you'll most likely suffer tons of regret. Discipline weighs ounces;

regret weighs tons. It's much easier to be disciplined and have the money than to try to rationalize why you don't. I'm telling you, better a few disciplines than a lack of dignity.

Don't wish for less problems; wish for more skills. Don't wish for less challenges; wish for more wisdom. Don't wish for it to change out there; develop yourself to the point that you can truly and totally rely on yourself. Develop yourself into self-reliance, which is the second part of building your ambition. In summary, self-reliance includes self-responsibility, counting on yourself, believing in yourself, doing it yourself, disciplining and encouraging yourself.

Now we're ready to move on to the third principle of building your ambition, which is self-discipline.

4

PRINCIPLE 3: SELF-DISCIPLINE

Of all the subjects we've covered so far, none is more important than the *disciplines for success*. What's at the core of achieving the good life?

The major key is not learning how to set goals or how to better manage your time or mastering the attributes of leadership. Every day in a thousand different ways, we are trying to improve ourselves by learning how to do things. We spend a lifetime gathering knowledge in classrooms, in textbooks, and experiences. But if knowledge is power and the forerunner to success, then why do we fall short of our objectives? Why, in spite of all our knowledge and our collective experiences, do we find ourselves aimlessly wandering through life, settling for existence rather than substance? There may be many answers to these two questions. Yours may be different from your associate's, spouse's, or friend's answers. While there may be many answers, the fundamental answer is the absence of discipline.

So to answer the very first question of this chapter, what's at the core of achieving the good life? The answer is consistent self-discipline. It doesn't really matter how smart you are or how much you know if you don't use that wisdom. It doesn't really matter that you graduated magna cum laude if you're stuck in a low-paying job. It doesn't really matter if you attended every seminar that comes to town if you don't apply what you've learned. Better than knowledge is the discipline to *apply* knowledge.

Once we've applied our knowledge, we must study the results of that process. Apply our knowledge, study the results, refine our approach. Finally, by trying, observing, refining, and trying again, our knowledge will inevitably produce worthy, admirable results. With the joy and results of our efforts, we continue to apply, learn, observe, and fuel our ambition with the positive reinforcement of continued progress. Soon we find that we're swept into a spiral of achievement, a vertical rise to success, and the ecstasy of that total experience makes for a life of triumph over tragedy, dullness, and mediocrity.

You will be swept into a spiral of achievement, a vertical rise to success, and the ecstasy of a life of triumph!

But for this whole process to work for us, we must first master the art of consistent self-discipline, including setting goals, time management, leadership, and parenting and relationships.

If we don't make consistent self-discipline part of our daily lives, the results we seek will be sporadic and elusive. It takes consistent effort to truly manage our valuable time, or we'll be consistently frustrated. Our time will be eaten up by others whose demands are stronger than our own.

It Takes Discipline To...

It takes discipline to conquer the nagging voices in our minds, the fear of failure, the fear of success, the fear of poverty, the fear of a broken heart. It takes discipline to keep trying when that nagging voice within brings up the possibility of failure. It takes discipline to admit our errors and recognize our limitations.

The voice of the human ego speaks to all of us. Sometimes the voice of ego says we should magnify our value beyond our results. It leads us to exaggerate, to not be totally honest. It takes discipline to be totally honest, both with ourselves and with others.

Be certain of one thing: every exaggeration of the truth, once detected by others, destroys our credibility and makes all that we say and do suspect. As soon as a business colleague realizes that we tend to exaggerate, guess what? That colleague thinks we always exaggerate and will never quite hold us in the same regard again—never.

Only an all-out, disciplined assault can overcome a bad habit.

The tendency to exaggerate, distort, or even withhold the truth is an inherent part of all of us, starting when we're kids. Johnny says, "I didn't do it. I didn't do it." Well, maybe Johnny didn't do it, but he probably had something to do with it. Then it continues when we're adults—exaggerating the benefits of a product to make a sale, exaggerating our net worth to impress old friends, exaggerating how close we are to closing a deal to impress the boss. Only an all-out, disciplined assault can overcome this tendency.

It takes discipline to change a habit, because habits are formed a little bit each day, every day. Once habits are formed, they act like a giant cable. They act like a nearly unbreakable instinct that only long-term disciplined activity can change. We must unweave every strand of the cable of habits slowly and methodically, until the cable that once held us in bondage is nothing more than scattered strands of wire.

It takes the consistent application of a new discipline—a more desirable one—to overcome one that is less desirable. It takes discipline to plan and execute our plan. It takes discipline to look with full objectivity at the results of our applied plan. It takes discipline to change either our plan or our method of executing that plan, if the results are poor.

It takes discipline to be firm when the world throws opinions at our feet. It takes discipline to ponder the value of someone else's opinion when our pride and our arrogance lead us to believe that we are the only ones with the answers. With this consistent discipline applied to every area of our lives, we can discover untold miracles and uncover unique possibilities and opportunities.

Because *self-discipline* is the key word, and discipline is the key action, then what exactly is discipline? One good answer might be that discipline is a constant human awareness of the need for action and a conscious act by us to implement that action. There-fore, *discipline is an awareness of the constant need for action and a conscious act to implement that action.* If our awareness and our implementations occur at the same time, then we begin a valuable sequence of disciplined activity.

Consistent discipline can reveal untold miracles and unique possibilities and opportunities.

Procrastination

Here's the other side of discipline. If considerable time passes between the moment of awareness and the time of our implementation, that is called procrastination. Procrastination is doing something—anything—tomorrow instead of today. Procrastination is an almost exact opposite of discipline. The voice within us says, "Get it done." Discipline says, "Do it now. Do it to the best of your ability today, tomorrow, and always until finally the worthy deed becomes instinctive." Procrastination says, "Later. Tomorrow. Whenever I get a chance." Procrastination also says, "Do what is necessary to get by or to impress others. Do what you can but not what you must."

In every circumstance we face, we are constantly presented with these two choices—do it now or do it later; discipline and procrastination; a choice between a disciplined existence bearing the fruits of achievement and contentment or procrastination, the easy life that will bear no fruit, only the bare branches of mediocrity.

An immediate reward for lack of discipline is a fun day at the beach.

The rewards of a disciplined life are great but are often delayed until sometime in the future. The rewards for the lack of discipline are immediate but minor compared to the immeasurable rewards of consistent self-discipline. An immediate reward for lack of discipline is a fun day at the beach. A future reward of discipline is owning the beach.

A future reward of discipline is owning the beach.

Most choose today's pleasure rather than tomorrow's fortune. So how can you get rid of the distractions? How can you keep your mind on what you're trying to do? How can you keep an attitude of doing it all and doing it now? How can you make the choice of discipline over procrastination? How can you stay focused on your ambitions? How can you avoid conversations at the watercooler?

You can focus on your work and finish it today, not tomorrow. You must work on your consistent self-discipline on a daily basis or you will be distracted by negative thoughts, negative people, and watercooler chatter. And depending on the type of people you associate with, you will be distracted by self-doubts. Never underestimate the power of influence and associations— and never underestimate the power of your own consistent self-discipline.

Three Steps to Becoming Disciplined

Let's take a closer look at the three steps to becoming disciplined: (1) true discipline is not the easiest option; (2) discipline is a full-time activity, day by day, every day; and (3) for every disciplined effort, there is a multiple reward.

First, true discipline is not the easiest option. Most people would rather sleep until 10:00 in the morning than get up at 6:00 a.m. It's easier to go to bed late, sleep late, show up late, and leave early than to have the discipline to do otherwise. It's easier not to read. It's easier to turn on the television than to open a book. It's easier to do just enough than to do it all. Waiting is always easier than acting. Trying is always easier than doing. Imagine what life would be like if we didn't have to make our bed in the morning, keep our clothes clean, pay our taxes, or show up for work tomorrow. Wouldn't it be fascinating if we didn't have to do these things? What do you suppose would become of us? You're right—not much.

For whatever the reason, the system we live in and contribute to is designed to make the easiest things in life the most unprofitable. Profitable seems to be the most difficult. Our world is and always will be a constant battle between the life of ease and its momentary rewards and a life of discipline and its far more significant rewards.

The price of discipline or the price of regret— you will pay one or the other.

Each has its own price—the price of discipline or the price of regret. We will pay one or the other. What we wish we had done is the voice of regret, speaking in a sorrowful tone at a time when there is no going back. This is regret, no second chance. What would we do differently? Choose one or the other, but both have a price to pay—the price of discipline or the price of regret. One costs pennies, the other a fortune.

Russian novelist and philosopher Fyodor Dostoevsky said, "There are hundreds of young men who would die for the truth but very few who would spend five years studying to know what the truth is." Dying for the truth is much more dramatic than the discipline of studying it one book at a time, one day at a time, one month at a time. But in the big picture, is dying for the truth really easier than adhering to the daily disciplines?

The first lesson of discipline is that it isn't the easiest option.

Second, discipline is a full-time activity. We've said that the best form of discipline is consistent self-discipline. The discipline that it takes to make your bed every day is the same discipline necessary for success in the world of business. The discipline to wash and dry your clothes is the same discipline to organize your business.

Consistency cannot be inconsistent.

All disciplines carry through to affect all parts of our lives. If we're disciplined in just one area and lazy in another, guess what? Soon the lazy side will creep in and destroy the disciplined side. The bad habits in one area of our life will eventually destroy our self-discipline in the areas we've been working on.

Consistency cannot be inconsistent. Discipline is the mind being trained to control our lives. Discipline is a set of standards we've selected as a personal code of conduct. Discipline is imposing on ourselves the requirements for honoring these standards. Once we've adopted these standards of behavior and conduct, we're committed to honor them. If we don't, there can be no disciplined activity.

Sometimes we may announce our standards to our relatives, friends, and associates. We shout our beliefs and condemn those who believe any differently, but we don't walk the talk. We end up acting in a way far different from the beliefs we've shouted. We tell our kids that the TV is rotting their minds, yet we spend our evenings in front of it. We tell our employees that they must take advantage of every minute of the working day, yet we spend three hours at lunch. *Do as I say, not as I do.* This is being inconsistent. This leads to a loss of credibility among those who watch us. More importantly, this leads to a loss of credibility within ourselves.

The only thing worse than one who is inconsistent in applying their self-imposed disciplines is one who has never considered the need or the value of discipline at all. These people seem to wander aimlessly, changing procedures, changing standards, changing loyalties, and shifting frequently from one commitment to another, leaving behind a trail of broken friendships, unfinished projects, and unfulfilled promises, all because of a discipline that was either nonexistent or imposed so infrequently that it was ineffective.

Here's the third step to becoming consistently self-disciplined. Number one is realizing that discipline isn't the easiest option. Number two is that self-discipline is a full-time activity, day by day, every day. *Third* is really a philosophy that holds one of life's unique promises: for every disciplined effort, there is a multiple reward. That's one of life's great arrangements. It's like the law of sowing and reaping. In fact, it's an extension of the biblical law that says, "If you sow well, you reap well."

A unique part of the law of sowing and reaping is that it not only suggests that we reap what we sow; it also suggests that we will reap much more. Life is full of laws that both govern and explain behaviors, but this may well be the major law we need to understand.

For every disciplined effort, there can be multiple rewards. What a concept! If you render unique service, your reward will be multiplied. If you're fair and honest and patient with others, your reward will be multiplied. If you give more than you expect to receive, your reward is more than you expect.

For every disciplined effort, there can be multiple rewards.

But remember, the key word is *discipline.* Everything of value requires care and attention. Everything of value requires discipline. Children require discipline through a structure and boundaries to work within so they feel secure and comfortable to explore and grow. They must learn to recognize what's right and what's wrong, what's acceptable behavior and what's not acceptable. Children require unwavering discipline, consistent discipline, or they'll be confused.

Likewise, our thoughts require discipline. We must set up our inner boundaries or our code of conduct and thoughts will be confused and we will become hopelessly lost in the maze of life.

Confused thoughts produce a state of confusion that affects our whole being.

Look around you at this very moment in time. What else may be vying for your attention? Perhaps you're reading in the living room on the sofa while the television is on. Maybe you're reading alone in your bedroom because you had a disagreement with someone you love and your anger keeps you hidden away from that person.

The most valuable form of discipline is the one you impose on yourself.

Wouldn't this be an ideal time to examine your need for a new discipline? Perhaps you're on the brink of giving up, or starting over, or starting out. The only missing ingredient to your incredible success story in the future is a new and self-imposed discipline that will make you stay longer, try harder, and work more intensely than you ever thought you possibly could.

The most valuable form of discipline is the one you impose on yourself. Don't wait for things to deteriorate so drastically that someone else must impose discipline on your life. Wouldn't that be tragic? How could you possibly explain the fact that someone else thought more of you than you thought of yourself that they forced you to get up early and get out into the marketplace?

Are you content to let success go to people who cared more about themselves than you care about yourself?

Our lives can serve as a warning of the consequences of neglect, self-pity, lack of direction, and ambition—or as an example of talent put to use, discipline self-imposed, and objectives clearly perceived and intensely pursued.

Too Much of a Good Thing?

Can too much discipline be bad? Can you possibly be too disciplined? Yes. Too much of anything is bad. Life without balance results in imbalance. Walking around the block every day is good. Walking or running six hours a day is bad. It's obsessive...unless, of course, you make your living as a marathon runner; then you're doing your job.

Eating an apple a day is good. Eating only apples is bad. You won't get all the protein and vitamins and nutrients your body needs. Working hard, burning the midnight oil, doing it "until" is good. Working nonstop, never taking a vacation, never having any fun, never spending quality time with the people you love is bad.

If you have your nose to the grindstone all the time, you will never spot new opportunities or consider new ideas. You have to stop and ponder where you've been and where you're going. You have to reflect so you know if you're even on the right track.

You have probably heard the story of Willy Loman in the play and movie *Death of a Salesman*. Willy was a workaholic. He typified the old-fashioned concept of success. After all, if you're always working, you must be successful. No, it doesn't work that way. For workaholics, there's never enough work. They can work 10, 12, 14 hours a day and work two jobs back to back. Their only satisfaction is fighting off sleep, denying life's pleasures, and completing more tasks.

Some people are impressed with this type of behavior, but just because a workaholic spends too much time working doesn't mean he or she ends up with the most money. These people are generally more task-oriented than results-oriented. They're busy being busy, not busy being productive. Workaholics generally end up alienating their families, losing their health, and facing a crisis of values.

Wouldn't you prefer a life of productivity rather than a life of tasks? Of course. When you schedule and take advantage of your time, you can work smarter instead of working longer. You'll probably end up getting more done than the workaholic and still have time for other things in life. Enlightened self-interest says, "I will look for new ways to work smarter by focusing on doing more per hour instead of doing more hours. I will run my day so my day doesn't run me." Enlightened self-interest also says that a life worth living comes from a life of balance and moderation. Too much of anything, even good things, will sooner or later throw you off track.

Visual Chain Thinking

The key technique you can use to keep yourself on the right track is a technique called visual chain thinking. Ambitious people don't see each step toward their goals as a single step, each discipline as a single discipline, each project as a single project, each sale as a single sale. With everything they do and every discipline they adhere to, they see it all as part of a chain—a link in the chain of events and actions that leads them to their final destination. Every action and every discipline today is a link in the chain. Every action and every discipline tomorrow is a link. Every action and every discipline in the future is a link. When you can see that every link in the chain eventually leads you to the things you want most out of life, to the person you want to become, you won't grow discouraged, fearful, or impatient with today. When you can see where you're going through visual chain thinking, even on the toughest days you'll keep building your power of ambition.

Part of visual chain thinking is built when you decide on your direction—when you can see where you're going to end up before you get there; for example, when you can see California while staring at the east side of a 14,000-foot mountain. Building your visual chain of thought begins when you have well-defined plans for your career, your family activities, your investments, and your health.

Your plans and goals are your visual chain, knowing where you're going before you get there. Develop a plan, a game plan. It's ironic how we all understand the importance of mapping out a strategy for a football game or a sales presentation. Not one professional team in the world begins a game without a complete strategy. But few of us take the time to map out a strategy, or game plan, for our lives—yet it's very important.

Game Plan Rules

Some game plan of life rules:

- Don't start your day until you have it finished.

- Don't begin your daily activities until you know exactly what you plan to accomplish.

- Don't start your day until you have it planned.

And do this every day. I know all this writing takes time and a disciplined effort, but remember that value is the fruitful result of discipline, not hope.

When you've mastered the art of planning your day, you're ready for the next level.

- Don't start your week until you have it finished.

- Don't begin your weekly activities until you know exactly what you plan to accomplish.

- Don't start your week until you have it planned.

Just imagine what life would be like if you took time out of every Sunday to plan your week. Come Friday, you won't be saying, "Boy did this week fly by. Where did it go? What do I do now?" No. If you plan your week before you start it, you'll know exactly what you want to do, what you want to accomplish, what you need to work on.

If you learn to plan your days as part of your overall game plan for the week, the parts will fit much better. Your days will be better, more effective. You'll be working smarter, not harder. When you've learned to plan your week, guess what? You have to plan your month. Don't start your month until it's finished.

By developing a game plan for your days, your weeks, your months—by developing and following your game plan—your days and weeks and months all become part of a bigger plan, a bigger design, a long-term view of your life, a visual chain. You gain a greater perspective of it all because you are planning. It takes great discipline on your part, but it will soon lead to a new habit—a habit of mastering your time, a habit of discipline that leads you to the good life.

Your Game Plan

Now, if visually seeing the future is new to you, if you've never developed a game plan, let me offer a few tips. There are two things you need to understand before you create a game plan.

1. A game plan, a visual chain of your future, is like a spreadsheet. Instead of listing numbers, you list activities. It's like a to-do list.

2. The technique of developing a game plan can be used for a single day, a single project, or a variety of projects that are happening simultaneously.

Here's how you do it. First of all, buy a pad of graph paper. Game plans work best on graph paper. On a sheet of graph paper, make vertical columns for the number of days this plan is to cover. Then on the left-hand side of the paper, write the heading "Activities." Under this heading, list all the activities to be accomplished within your time frame.

Let's say, for example, that you have one week to finalize a marketing plan. It's an overwhelming amount of work to complete, but it has to be done. Break it down piece by piece. The

95

best way to start is by listing all of the individual components on the left-hand side of the page. Some may need to be completed before others can be started. For example, you have to have your market research results compiled before you can determine your target market. You need to know your target market before you can develop your marketing strategy. You need to have your marketing strategy before you can create a budget for collateral materials, and so on. When you break down the project piece by piece, deadline by deadline, you can be more effective in delegating the appropriate pieces of the puzzle and more effective in doing your own work while orchestrating the rest.

It's an incredible feeling to be in charge of your life, your surroundings, your future.

The final result of developing a visual chain, your game plan, is a clear visual presentation of the tasks before you. Keep your game plan in plain sight. Post it in your office where you can easily read it. Have a copy at home and tape it to the refrigerator. Keep a copy in your journal for quick reference.

Your game plan serves as a constant reminder of all you need to do to get where you want to go. If you're doing all that you're scheduled to do, game plans are very rewarding. The discipline of developing and following a game plan is exciting. Day by day by day, week by week by week, month by month by month, you'll see the magic of your dreams and plans turning into reality. It's an incredible feeling to be in charge of your life, your surroundings, your future.

Better Than a Work of Art

It's like creating a work of art on the biggest canvas imaginable. It's creative. It's beautiful. It is exciting to dream a dream, plan for the dream, and then watch your dream turn into reality. What's really powerful about creating game plans is that you can see your future right before your eyes.

On the days when your energy isn't up to par, your enthusiasm is a little low, your ambition isn't pulling you forward, and your attitude isn't on the high side, use your game plan to see how far you've come and take time to realize just exactly where you're headed. On the days you're disciplined, your visual chain of the future will pull you ahead.

Oh, and make sure your game plan includes more than work projects. There should be times for recreation, reflection, exercise, healthy activities and eating, and time for spirituality. Let's say you've developed your plan and you've penciled in writing a report from 9:00 a.m. to 10:00 a.m. Well, what if you don't do your best report writing this early in the morning? What if you do this kind of work best at 3:00 in the afternoon? Know yourself well enough to know what you do best at different times of the day, week, month, etc. Know the best time for you to accomplish a certain type of task, and schedule it during those times. You have to work your game plan to best work for you.

In the end, it is your own discipline that is the best, most effective catalyst to give substance and depth to your ambition. To achieve your own plans and dreams, to have what you want to have, and to become what you want to become, your consistent self-discipline is the key. The ultimate question cannot be whether you are going to make the fundamental disciplines your own; the ultimate question is *when*.

With intense and consistent application of worthy disciplines, we have the individual and collective capacity to change ourselves, our incomes, our attitudes, our lifestyles, and our effect on other people. We can change opinions. We can change leadership. We can even change the direction of our nation. We have the opportunity. We have the capacity. We have the answers, and we have the ability. The elements are all there, including the freedom to try—only the discipline is missing. That element, and the decision to use it, lies within all of us. The choice is ours.

5

PRINCIPLE 4: SELF-ENTERPRISE

So far, we've discussed the three principles of building your ambition: (1) positive self-direction, knowing who you are and where you want to go; (2) self-reliance, taking responsibility for your own life, taking full responsibility for whatever happens to you; and (3) self-discipline, creating the need for action and implementing that action every day until it becomes a way of life, a good habit.

Now we explore the fourth principle of building your ambition—*self-enterprise*, building your enterprising skills to consistently create new opportunities. Self-enterprise is to consistently take advantage of the opportunity you create, to be aware, to face life with your eyes and ears open to the possibilities that may be just around the corner. An enterprising person, for example, comes across a pile of scrap metal and sees the making of a wonderful sculpture.

To be enterprising is to keep your eyes open and your mind active.

An enterprising person drives through an old, decrepit part of town and sees a new housing development. An enterprising person sees opportunity in all areas of life. To be enterprising is to keep your eyes open and your mind active and to be skilled, confident, creative, and disciplined enough to seize opportunities that present themselves, regardless of the economy.

An enterprising mortgage banker will develop creative financing strategies during slow markets. An enterprising lawyer will study new laws and market to people who may need help in those areas. Enterprising salespeople will research beyond the obvious to find new prospects for the products or services, isolate a secondary market, and develop another benefit.

An enterprising mind and attitude researches before taking action, is resourceful, and does everything possible in preparation for what's to come.

Think of a few people you know who are enterprising—think of people in the news, in your office, in your neighborhood. What do these people have in common?

- They are most times on the go, developing a plan, following a plan, reworking the plan until it fits.

- They are probably very resourceful, never letting anything get in their way.

- They probably don't understand the word "no" when it applies to their visions of the future.

- When posed with a problem, they probably say, "Let's figure out a way to make it work" instead of, "It won't work."

- Self-enterprising people always see the future in the present.

- Self-enterprising people always find a way to take advantage of a situation, not be burdened by it.

- Self-enterprising people aren't lazy.

- They don't wait for opportunities to come to them; they go after the opportunities. Self-enterprise means always finding a way to keep yourself actively working toward your ambition.

Creativity and Courage—Two Components of Self-Enterprise

Self-enterprise requires creativity and courage.

Creativity to see what's out there and shape it to your advantage. Creativity to look at the world a little differently. Creativity to take a different approach. Creativity to be different.

Courage goes hand in hand with the creativity: The courage to be creative. The courage to see things differently. The courage to go against the crowd. The courage to take a different approach. The courage to stand alone if you have to. The courage to choose activity over ease. And activity generally relates to how you feel about yourself—understanding your self-worth, how valuable you are.

What could you do if you had all the skills, took the classes, read the books, burned the midnight oil? What could you do? What true value could you develop? This is one of the better exercises to really examine yourself and your potential. Think seriously about the following questions and your answers:

- What could I become?

- What could I really do in the marketplace?

- How valuable could I become in enterprise, home, family, experience, love, friendship, marriage, and overall?

- Am I valuable enough to work on what's not working so I can reach my full capacity?

- If I'm operating at 20 percent, what could I possibly do with the other 80 percent?

When you understand how valuable you are, it's a whole new experience. Understanding self-worth plays a major role in our ability to be self-enterprising. Our self-worth makes the difference between being lazy and being active, being self-enterprising. If we don't feel good about ourselves, we won't feel good about our lives. And if we don't feel good about our lives, we won't be very interested in looking for opportunities.

Being self-enterprising isn't only about the ability to make money. Self-enterprising also means feeling good about yourself and having a great enough self-worth to want to seek advantages and opportunities that will make a difference in the future.

Do More, Not Less

Enterprise is always better than ease. Every time we choose to do less than we possibly can, it affects our self-confidence and self-worth. If we *do* a little less every day, we are also *being* a little less every day. Can you imagine what you would be like after ten years of doing a little less every day? Being less than you can be is devastating. Think about it. Doing less can ruin your life.

103

You can reverse the process of doing a little less by doing more—by using your self-direction, self-reliance, and self-discipline. You alter the course by doing a little more each day. And soon you develop a new habit of doing rather than neglecting. Consistently doing more will increase your confidence, courage, creativity, and self-worth. In the end, it's how we feel about ourselves that provides us with the increased courage and creativity for self-enterprise.

How we feel about ourselves provides the greatest reward from activity and enterprise. It's not what we get or what we accumulate that makes us valuable; it's what we become. Success isn't in the having; success is in the doing. The process of doing that brings value. The activity that transforms our dreams into reality converts ideas into actuality. Self-enterprise is found in the activity; without activity, we miss the opportunity.

Success isn't in the having; success is in the doing.

Let me tell you what I think most messes with the mind—doing less than you can. Doing less causes all kinds of mental damage. Being less than you can be, trying less, and doing with less enthusiasm messes with the mind. It damages our self-image because the minute we turn this around and start extending ourselves, we see immediate rewards—maybe not monetary right away, but how you feel about yourself is instant and that's the greatest value.

It's not what we get that makes us valuable; it's what we become. Discover all you can do, see how much you can earn, can share, can start, can finish, can reach, and how far you can extend your influence. I have no doubt you will be amazed!

Better and Better

Some people would have us believe that positive affirmation is more important than activity. Instead of doing something constructive to change our lives, they repeat slogans and canned affirmations like "Every day and in every way, I'm getting better and better." Well, getting better and better doesn't just happen from wishful thinking. Getting better and better only happens with the discipline of doing better and better. Discipline is the requirement for progress. And affirmations without discipline are, in reality, delusions.

Now don't get me wrong here—there's nothing wrong with affirming the good life, as long as we are disciplined enough to take action. Affirmations can be effective as long as we remember two very important rules: number one, we should never allow affirmation to replace action, activity, enterprise—*feeling* better is no substitute for *doing* better—and number two, whatever we choose to affirm must be the truth. If the truth happens to be that we're broke, the best affirmation would be to simply say, "I'm broke," face it, accept it, be responsible for it, and change it. By admitting out loud that you're broke, you'll probably be disgusted enough to start the thinking process about how to change it. Anyone saying, "I'm broke" with conviction will most likely be driven from ease into action.

Facing reality is always the best beginning.

Confronting harsh realities has an incredible effect on the mind. Confronting the truth and then applying the discipline to express the truth, instead of disguising it, inevitably leads to positive change. And reality is always the best beginning. Within reality lies the possibility to create our own personal miracles. The power of faith starts with reality. If we can bring ourselves to state the truth about a situation, then, as the saying goes, "The truth will set us free." Here's another profound saying: "Faith isn't faith unless it's all you're holding on to."

If your life and circumstances have resulted in an ugly situation, call it ugly. If you've lost it all, admit you've lost it all; be responsible for it. And if faith is all you have left, use it; create your own personal miracle. When we understand and accept the truth, the promise of the future is freed from the shackles of deception. When we accept the truth, the promise of the future will pull us forward.

Creative Techniques to Keep on Track

Remember, creativity is the first requirement for self-enterprise. The following are six creative techniques to keep you on the right track toward that promising future of self-enterprise: (1) think on paper; (2) develop your brainstorming ability; (3) imagine outlandish solutions; (4) use doodles, flow charts, and formulas; (5) access the information highway; and (6) commit yourself to learning.

Number one: *Think on paper.*

You can't take a trip to somewhere new without a roadmap. You can't build a house with the plans in your head. You can't build a company with the business plan in your head. You can't seek venture capital with the financials in your head. But you *can* put it all on paper—your roadmap, blueprints, business plan, financial projections—so you can analyze your path, solve your problems, and isolate what works and what doesn't.

You can use this technique for your life as well. If you're faced with a mental roadblock, write it all down on paper. Like we discussed previously, when you put a problem on paper, you take the emotion out of it. With the emotion gone, you can look at the roadblock objectively. You can figure out what you did right and what you did wrong and how to change it.

So, pick a problem out of your head and pull out a piece of paper. Then draw a line down the middle. On the left-hand side, jot down what the problem is; write it out. We have so much going on in our heads that we can't figure things out until we take a piece of it out and put it on paper. State the problem the best you can.

On the right-hand side of the paper, write all the possible solutions that come to mind. I ask myself three questions to find the answers. And by the way, these three questions can be used to solve almost any problem.

The first question you need to write down: *What can I do?* You may be able to solve the problem yourself. Jot down all the possible solutions, and then analyze each one. Is one better than another? Look at all the alternatives of each solution, and write down everything you discover.

The second question to ask yourself: *What can I read to solve my problem?* Maybe someone with the same problem wrote a book with the solution that will work for you. Maybe it's written out in concise language somewhere to give you the instant benefit of someone's advice. You don't need to reinvent the wheel. Do your homework and find the solution.

First try to find the answer yourself, from your own experience. If you can't find it yourself, then ask, *What could I read?* Go to the bookstore, search your own library, go back through your journals or files to find what's been helpful and valuable to you in the past. Maybe you made some notes that could be helpful. Research on the Internet, looking specifically for credible sources. Then analyze and write down all of what you found, and implement what solves the problem.

The third question to ask yourself: *Who can I ask?* When approaching someone who is knowledgeable about your type of problem, you can present all your carefully analyzed paperwork as a starting point for discussion.

I promise you if you try these ideas and ask these questions when you have a problem, you can solve about anything that gets in your way.

Number two: *Develop your brainstorming ability.*

What is brainstorming? Just what it sounds like—allowing your brain to go in any and all directions, to be free from inhibitions and objections and negatives. Brainstorming is putting an idea into your brain and letting it take off, free associating; not planning a train of thought, but thinking freely.

If you're planning a creative strategy session with your associates, a brainstorming session, let me give you a little hint: effective brainstorming can only happen if you're free from your ego. You can't be worried about saying something stupid or silly or something totally off the wall—because your so-called silly thought may trigger someone else's brain to take it one step further and a brilliant stroke of genius will emerge.

Brainstorming in a group is an experience of collective thought, an experience of developing one idea or several ideas through a variety of thought processes. Here's another hint: brainstorming can't be effective unless everyone involved is comfortable with each other. If you don't feel comfortable within the group, you may withhold the very thought that provides the solution to the problem because you don't want to appear stupid.

How do you think all the advertisements you see on TV and in the magazines get created? How do you think some of those crazy campaigns are born? The process happens through hours and hours of creative brainstorming and working papers. Every member of the team jots down notes, and one idea builds on another idea and another and another. And pretty soon, a campaign is born out of the collective thoughts of the group.

I don't believe that the best decisions are made by committee, but great ideas are often created by committee. Brainstorming can often lead you to solutions you would never have thought of if you imposed parameters on your thought process.

Number three: *Imagine outlandish solutions.*

Get your brain out of the ruts by considering ideas without considering their practicality. If you allow yourself to think without confinement, you may come across a solution that seems totally inappropriate. But this type of thinking allows you to open up the process, which will eventually lead to totally appropriate solutions.

Number four: *Use doodles, flow charts, and formulas.*

That's right—doodling. What got you in trouble in grade school is actually quite stimulating to the brain. The way you think while doodling is quite different from the way you think while creating a flow chart or writing a formula. Your doodles may end up looking like some symbol that will trigger your brain to think of an alternative solution. Drawing creative doodles wakes up a different part of your brain.

Create a flow chart showing the path to success. What does it look like? Is it a straight course? A varied course? Does it have a lot of curves and corners and different angles? Try creating a flow chart to success. It doesn't matter if it is accurate or not. What matters is that it's stimulating the creative thought process.

Formulas work the same way. When you awaken that creative part of you, you'll be amazed at the opportunities that were always there, ones you never saw before. It's all a matter of how you look at life and opportunities.

Number five: *Access the information highway.*

It's amazing the kind of information you can find on the Internet. At the touch of your keyboard you have access to millions of responses to any type of question. You can access stock quotes, worldwide newspapers. You can research anything and everything. You can call up a bulletin board and directly ask questions of other users. You can make numerous new contacts and develop an entirely new network, or several.

From the electronic age, computer age, information age, digital age, or technology age—no matter what you call this time in history—access to limitless information and communication is vital. Resources available for common use have totally changed the ways people and businesses interact. If you don't take full advantage of all the available opportunities to connect and network locally, nationally, and internationally, you will quickly be outmaneuvered.

Number six: *Commit yourself to learning.*

Feed your mind, sharpen your interest in two major subjects— life and people. Learn how to better interact with others. Learn how to get the most from life. Learn all you can so you can become all you can become.

Learning is the essence of a life worth living. That includes self-enterprise, wealth, happiness, good health, spirituality, and faith. Learning and searching is where the process of creating your own personal miracle begins.

Let's review. There are six steps to creatively build your self-enterprise traits and ultimately build and use your power of ambition:

1. Think on paper; write what you need to remember.

2. Develop the ability to brainstorm.

3. Imagine outlandish solutions to your challenges.

4. Doodles, flow charts, and formulas will spur your thought processes.

5. Access the information highway; use all resources available.

6. Commit yourself to learning; learn all you can to become all you can become.

Courage

Now we will focus on the second component of self-enterprise—courage. Ambition requires courage to stand up for what's right and fight what's wrong. Ambition requires that you hold on to your values in pursuit of your success and that you fight off fear. Fear is an emotion that can stop people dead in their tracks, foregoing success and achievement. Fear can stop people from taking all that life has to offer them. Fear can rear its ugly head in many ways.

You can be afraid of success. You can be afraid of failure. You can be afraid of looking ridiculous. You can be afraid of change, either positive or negative. You can be afraid of competition. You can be afraid of loss and destruction. There are only two innate fears humans are born with: the fear of falling and the fear of loud sounds.

"The only thing we have to fear is fear itself."

—President Franklin D. Roosevelt

So what about our learned fears? Maybe some of your fears are brought on by your own experiences, by what someone has told you, by the news you've read. Some fears are valid, like walking alone in a crime-ridden part of town at 2:00 in the morning. If there isn't fear, there's probably a bit of ignorance. And that type of ignorance can easily be solved by either education or experience. When you learn to avoid that situation, you won't live in fear of it.

Fears, even the most basic ones, can totally destroy our ambitions. Fear can destroy fortunes, relationships, business opportunities, to name just a few. Fear, if left unchecked, can destroy our lives. Fear is an enemy.

Fears and Enemies

We also face enemies on the inside. One of those enemies you have to destroy before it destroys you is *indifference*. What a tragic disease this is: "Ho-hum, let it slide." Then soon you are drifting, drifting away from your ambitions.

The next enemy inside all of us is *indecision*. Indecision is called the thief of opportunity, the thief of self-enterprise. Not making decisions will steal your chances for a better future. Take a sword to the enemy of indecision.

Another inside enemy is *doubt*. Sure, there's room for healthy skepticism; you can't believe everything, but don't let doubt take over your mind. Don't doubt the past, the future, each other, the government, the possibilities and opportunities—and don't doubt yourself. Doubt will destroy your life, your chances for success. Doubt can empty your bank account and your heart. Doubt is an enemy. Go after it; get rid of it.

Next is *worry*. We all worry sometimes, but don't let it conquer or alarm you unnecessarily. Worry can be useful to head off panic. For example, it's 3:00 in the morning and your teenager is not home yet—you worry. Worry allows you to think of all the possible scenarios, and hopefully you land on one that keeps you from becoming terrified. You worry, but don't let worry loose like a mad dog driving you into a small corner, fearing for your life. On the contrary, drive your worries into a small corner and crush them with common sense, with research, or by talking about it with someone.

Drive your worries into a small corner and crush them with common sense.

Whenever worry seems out to get you, work it out of your mind. Whatever's pushing on you, push back. Worried about illness? Determine to keep to your healthy living routine and discipline, and have the power to say, "I'm not going to let that happen. I'm going to fight illness like an enemy. I'll work on my health plan enough to destroy illness."

The next enemy inside is being *overcautious*—taking the timid approach to life. Timidity is not a virtue; it's an illness. And if you let it go and go and go, it will win and you will be without a promotion. Timid people don't get promoted. They don't advance

115

and grow and become powerful in the marketplace. It's possible to conquer timidity.

Do battle with the enemy and your fears. Do battle—build your courage to fight what's holding you back, keeping you from using the power of your ambition. Do battle—have the courage to fight back. Be courageous in your pursuit of what you want and who you want to become.

Build Your Courage

The following are a few techniques to help build your courage.

Number one, *put all remote possibilities out of your mind.* Don't worry about things you have no control over. Don't spend your time thinking about all the bad things that might happen to you. Don't spend your time plotting and planning ways to make sure these things will never happen to you. Courageous people don't worry about the unlikely things out of their control. They concentrate on what they *can* control.

Number two, *face your fears before you start a project.* Imagine difficult situations before they occur. Make a list of the worst that could happen, and you'll probably see that it's not so bad after all. A friend of mine lost everything a few years back: home, cars, possessions, antiques, art, jewelry, credit—lost it all. So now on her way back up, whenever she's faced with a tough decision, she asks herself, "What's the worst that can happen?" And guess what? She's already been through the worst and survived, so it's not an issue anymore.

You don't have to lose everything to lose that particular fear. But once you face your fear, you can move on. Once you've detailed the worst that could possibly happen, you'll see that you have the inner strength to deal with it.

When you look at the possibilities beforehand, most likely you will not be faced with the situation at all. Why? Because you've already thought it through, and by contemplating what might happen, you will chart your course to make sure it doesn't occur.

So, the first courage-building technique is to put the remote possibilities out of your mind. The second, to face fears beforehand.

Number three is to imagine the alternative. See in your mind the end result of giving in to your fear. Really feel the cost of being ruled by fear. Then, really feel the gain of following your ambition courageously. Weigh the two and feel the difference. If you've been invited to address your national sales convention and are scared to death of public speaking, what should you do? Well, you could decline the invitation, knowing full well that your fears are holding you back. Or you can take public speaking classes, read books, practice in front of a video camera and see yourself stepping up to a whole new league, gaining more notoriety in your field, increasing your opportunities for future success.

Once again, it's your choice. You can be frozen by your fears or face your fears and move forward. It all depends on if you can live with yourself always being afraid to take action. When you plot out your course for success, you know there will be some touchy moments when fear may get the best of you. But remember, if you use your visual chain thinking and can see your future ahead of you, if you really want what you're going after in pursuit of what you'll become, if you really believe in the power of ambition, then you know that true success comes from taking the enterprising route.

PRINCIPLE 5: WORKING WITH OTHERS

The fifth principle for building and using your power of ambition revolves around working with others. That your ability to work with others has an effect on building your ambition may sound a bit like a paradox, a contradiction, especially since I've stressed self-reliance and taking personal responsibility for all you do. But a successful life does involve other people: family, associates, kids, parents, employees, friends.

Working and living and spending time with other people means that you must take responsibility for your relationships. For instance, how many executives would be totally lost without their personal assistants? Quite a few. They're a team. One takes the spotlight; the other is invaluable behind the scenes. One is a great idea person; the other, a great detail person. Together they work to accomplish the mission of the company.

Of course, you need to be responsible for yourself and to yourself before you can be responsible to another person. You need to be the best you can be so you can bring your absolute best to every relationship. And that's the tie-in to using the power of your ambition so you can build mutually beneficial relationships. Remember, you can't be successful by yourself.

With that in mind, let's look at ways to build healthy relationships. Most of these tips are for building business relationships, contacts, and good working relationships with colleagues, vendors, prospects, and future, present, and past clients. But remember, we are all people with the same desires, regardless of our profession. Many of these tips work well for building other relationships too. Let's start with kindness.

Tips for Building Relationships

Be Kind

How kind should you be? As kind as you possibly can to everyone you come in contact with, including store clerks, people on the street, in your office, at home—everyone. Why? A kind word goes a long way to brighten someone's day. You may not know the clerk at the store is having a bad day, but when you offer up a smile with a kind word, a friendly, "Hello, how are you today? Nice weather we're having," you may be the only one that day who took the time to be kind. Maybe take a minute or two to listen to what someone has to say.

Kindness is an investment in others, which may come back to you multiplied.

Your few words of kindness and attention can turn somebody's day around, make them feel more worthwhile, cared for. Be generous with your kindness. It'll go a long way. People will remember, whether you know each other or not. If you're dining at a busy restaurant and you're especially nice to your server, you're investing in that person because it's the nice thing to do. As a benefit, but not the only intention, that server will remember you and you'll enjoy good service the next time you dine there. Kindness is an investment in others, which may come back to you multiplied. Kindness is so important in every aspect of your life, especially in building good relationships with others.

Be Sensitive

Sensitivity is being touched by the experiences of others, being sensitive to others' problems, understanding their plight, opening your heart and mind and attention to address the needs of others. Being sensitive is recognizing other people's feelings, putting yourself in someone else's shoes. If you sense a problem, be sensitive enough to ask some questions to get through to the root of the problem. Most people won't reveal the problem on the first question. When probing, be sensitive, not invasive or nosey.

You say, "Mary, how are you today? How are things?"

"Well, everything's okay."

And you can tell by the way she responded that everything's not okay. Most don't want to reveal the real problem unless (1) they are talking to someone they can trust and (2) they are talking to someone they believe really cares. So sometimes it takes a second or maybe a third or fourth question before trust builds and they know you do care. Then they're willing to tell you what's really going on. It saves so much time asking questions up front. Learn to ask questions that will build trust and communication between you and those with whom you want to establish a relationship. Learn how to *express* sincerity from the heart rather than try to *impress*.

Identify and Create Rapport

Strive to express your thoughts and philosophies and experiences so the person can relate to you and say, "Me too! I know exactly what you mean." When meeting someone for the first time, you're simply getting acquainted, making contact. First start by finding something you have in common, something you can both identify with. Start with where they are before you try taking them where you want them to go.

Again, asking questions is a good way to identify commonalities. Perhaps ask where they attended college, or what part of the country they grew up in, or why they chose their particular profession. Those are good jumping-off points to more in-depth and meaningful discussions. When the person identifies with you, a bridge is being built, and then you can start building rapport. Rapport is when you nurture a close bond from understanding each other.

Ensure Effective Communication

When you start building rapport or want to enhance rapport in the business world, you need effective communication skills that help you work better with others to achieve their goals and to achieve your goals. The following are a few tips on good communication, because to get along well, to work well, to live well with others, you must be a good communicator.

1. *Have something worth saying*—interesting, fascinating, sensitive, wise, good, etc.

2. *Say it well*—people must be able to understand what you're saying so you keep their attention and they realize what you are saying benefits them.

3. *Have a good delivery system* for your substance, and knowledge, and awareness, and understanding, and experience. Learn to say it well.

4. *Communicate with sincerity.* The best communication occurs when both people are sincere—one sincerely wishing to learn or listen and the other sincerely wishing to share.

5. *Repetition and practicing your communication skills* are keys to communicating well. Know what you need to say, and then practice, practice, practice. Practice is just as valuable as a sale because your communication skills are so valuable. *The sale will make you a living; your skills will make you a fortune.* So practice your presentation and your ability to communicate what you know.

Likewise, if you just talk, you can hold a family together. If you skillfully talk, you can build dreams and the future for everyone in the family. The difference is skill. You can cut down a tree with a hammer, but it takes about 30 days. If you trade the hammer for an ax, you can cut down the same tree in about 30 minutes. The difference between the 30 minutes and 30 days is the tool. And your best communication tool is your skill. So practice to get the skill of saying it well. Part of saying it well is sincerity. The next part is repetition.

6. *Brevity* is another tip for good communication. The more you know, the more concise you can be because your words are more effective. Jesus was brief when He was putting His team together. As He wandered the countryside, every once in a while

He saw someone He wanted on His team and said, "You, follow Me." Now, that's brief! Why could Jesus be so brief and yet be so effective? I think it is because His reputation preceded Him. When you become wiser, stronger, and have built a good reputation, when you arrive on the scene, your reputation may have preceded you. So when you arrive, you don't have to say much. You don't have to launch into a two-hour harangue. If your good reputation precedes you, a lot of the job is done before you ever step into the room.

7. Part of saying it well is *style*. Be a student of style, a variety of styles that you have researched and learned from successful others. Then make sure you develop your own. Be a student, but develop your own. Don't be someone else. Let someone else influence you, but don't become them. Develop your own style that fits you and you will communicate well

8. *You need a good vocabulary* to say it well. If you lack a substantial vocabulary, you're lacking the tools to describe what you need to communicate. You can't communicate without the words needed to convey the facts about your product, solutions to problems, or thoughts and ideas. And you can't communicate well without a defined vocabulary. Every time you come across a word that's new to you, look it up. Every time you're in a conversation and the other person uses a word that's new to you, look it up. Most of the time you can figure out the meaning of a new word by how it's used. But if you can't, make sure you hold your response until you know for sure the meaning.

Several years ago, some of my friends took a survey among prisoners for some rehabilitation program they were working on. They weren't actually looking for this result, but here's what they found: there was definitely a relationship between vocabulary and behavior. Interesting. The more limited the person's vocabulary, the more the tendency toward poor behavior. Wow. When you stop to think about it for a moment, it makes sense. Vocabulary is a way of seeing, it gives people insight into society, culture, education, prosperity, politics, success—everything. And only with the vocabulary people have can they see the world surrounding them. You can't use tools you don't have to see; to create light, understanding, awareness, comprehension, perception, vision. You can only have as much vision as your present vocabulary gives you. And if your vocabulary is limited, you can't see very well. Having a limited vocabulary is like seeing the world through a tiny hole. Can you imagine the judgment mistakes a person would make? Having a limited vocabulary limits understanding.

You have only as much vision as your present vocabulary gives you.

Vocabulary is a tool to express what's going on in our heart and our head; to translate our questions and answers and perceptions; what we see, to be able to say it. If you have a limited way of translating and expressing what's going on inside, you'll fall way behind.

Without a comprehensive vocabulary, people are unable to see the world or express themselves. Consequently, their world keeps getting smaller and smaller without vision and tools. Eventually, they don't need a place much bigger than 10 by 12 square feet in which to live. Why? That's about as big as their world is— just a small, narrow place, because they can't comprehend what's going on or understand the meaning of events because they have no tools (no necessary vocabulary words) with which to translate.

9. *"Reading" your audience* is also an important part of communicating well. You need to interpret what's going on between you and the people you're talking to. Maybe they would be more engaged if you spoke a little softer or stronger? Should you explain it more? Should you be clearer and more concise? Should you quit? A lot of the decision-making going on during a conversation depends on how well you can read, how well you can tell what's going on in the minds of those you're trying to reach. It doesn't matter if you're looking into the face of a child, a colleague, or a thousand faces in an audience, you have to read what's going on; you have to pay attention.

The following are some ways to read your audience.

The first one is to *read what you see.* Search the faces of your audience to see if you are being understood. See if they look perplexed and aren't understanding. Body language tells us a lot. Notice how the people are sitting, what they're doing with their hands, their eyes. Is someone's arms and legs crossed, chin tucked down and frowning? You have your work cut out for you. This person is not going to be easy to reach. Someone stands up from behind the desk? You have to hurry—the person is not going to listen to much more of what you have to say.

Also, *read what you hear.* You have to be a good listener to be a good communicator. Listen for feedback, which is so valuable. What you hear may help you change gears, be a little stronger, be a little softer, find a different illustration. *This one isn't working.* Search for another way to say it. Become sensitive to someone else's words, not just by preparing to talk when the other person is through. Listen. Pick up those signals that the feedback of words gives us.

Learn to *read your emotion* and what others are feeling so you can adjust your communication, approach, delivery, and can get your message across successfully. Communication is the key ingredient in being able to work well with others and to using the power of our ambition to welcome a fantastic future.

Applying Communication Skills

Now it's time to discuss how to best apply your communication skills, including what you can and can't do in the marketplace. How you talk and act while playing volleyball or golfing on a Saturday afternoon probably isn't the same way you would talk and act around a group of people who want to invest in your company. How you communicate with your friends and family is probably an abbreviated version of how you should communicate in a high-powered business setting.

When you meet a new group of people, first watch, listen, and be alert before you decide on the appropriate communication style. You might greet old friends with a slap on the back and a tasteless joke, but you certainly wouldn't greet a multimillion-dollar opportunity that way.

Take a few moments to study the temperament of your audience. Listen to how they communicate with each other. Watch how they react to situations and comments. Study your audience to avoid engaging in inappropriate behavior, which could prove costly. Some people could make about $150,000 a year, but they have to be satisfied with about $50,000 because of their improper behavior. They have the skills, but their behavior is costing them, keeping them set aside.

Costly Mistakes

Let's talk about communication mistakes in the marketplace that might cost you more than you want to pay.

Bad language will cost you. Some language is best kept in the sports bar rather than in the marketplace. Inappropriate language will have costly consequences. Cussing and telling dirty jokes in the marketplace will offend most professionals. They won't want to have you around to tarnish the company's reputation. And what happens then? It'll cost you.

Bad language also includes using business-specific lingo with people not familiar with the terminology. Your industry's buzzwords are just that—your industry's. People who speak computer language have to learn to shift gears when they step out of the office. Be careful not to use lingo when having a conversation with someone not in the same line of work.

Become a good judge of character or it may cost you. In the marketplace, there are sheep and wolves. We must be wise and understand that some wolves are so clever that they have learned to dress up like sheep. Do not miss the full-drama life story of good and evil. We must always be aware, sensitive, understanding;

know the scenarios; and be alert for the inevitable. We must learn to be a good judge of character so as not to succumb to a dastardly scheme or plot against us.

Being late will cost you. In some circles, it's acceptable, but most people view being late as being disrespectful of their time. They will think that if you're disrespectful of their time, you may be disrespectful of their business too. Why? Everything affects everything. Now, if you have a legitimate reason and your reputation is one of being punctual, then you might get away with it a time or two, but don't be late. One day you just may be too late to close the deal. Be on time.

Delivering criticism and expressing anger inappropriately can cost you. It's inevitable during the course of working with others that some situation will result in anger or some criticism that needs to be handed down. It's just part of life.

What do you do with your anger? You can't lash out at your children or your friends or your colleagues. But you can and must lash out at the problem or the situation. You say to your teenager, "You know I love you, but what you did was wrong. I hate it that you took the car without asking first. And I especially hate that you got a speeding ticket. What were you thinking?" So whatever the punishment, punish the bad deed, not the person.

Your assistant sends the contract to the seller instead of to the buyer. Make sure your assistant knows that you appreciate the work but not the wrongdoing. Whatever criticism you hand down, whatever anger you're processing, make sure that the person who receives it knows full well that you care but hate the error. If you're too steamed up at the moment to be rational, don't say anything until you've cooled off a bit.

In Dale Carnegie's book *The Leader in You*, he describes the attributes of kind criticism. He quotes Andrés Navarro's technique of kind criticism as the three-for-one rule. If you don't like something about the way someone works, write down the problem. But before you confront that person with criticism, discover three good things about the person. Noticing three good things gives you the right to criticize one bad thing. Interesting thought—criticism after appreciation.

With well-delivered and well-chosen words, you can admonish the doing without admonishing the doer. This is important. You love the person; you hate the act. Make sure they know the difference. You don't have to couch the words; you don't have to hide your anger or disappointment, but you do have to make sure that your communication is effective so that the wrongdoing will not be repeated.

The more you care, the stronger you can be. This has to do with intensity—the intensity of your communication with those you work with, live with, and are close to. If you really care for someone, they'll give you room to use powerful language—*if* they know you really care. When they know that and trust you, sticky problems can be solved and you can attack the dark side of bad behavior.

Effective Networking

Now that we've discussed the communication skills, let's move on to see how to translate these skills into creating more business. Networking is working within a group of people we know and/or working within a group of people we want to know. Let's examine some techniques for effective networking.

1. When developing relationships through networking, they must be mutually beneficial. The favor you do for someone else is expected to be returned someday. For each contact you give someone else, you expect one in return. For each tip you give out, you expect one in return. Or as the law of sowing and reaping says, it'll come back to you multiplied. That's number one: make sure your networking relationships are mutually beneficial.

2. *Keep the relationship active.* Schedule quarterly lunches. Plan to meet at chamber of commerce networking events. If you see a story about your contact in the newspaper, clip it out and send it with a note of congratulations. Send articles that may be relevant to the person's career. Keep in touch. Don't just call when you need something.

3. *Express your gratitude and appreciation.* Make it clear that you appreciate the contact or tip that was sent your way. Send a finder's fee if your latest deal was the result of your contact. Send a special gift if a tip panned out. A man I know got a stock tip in passing from an acquaintance of his, and the stock made him thousands of dollars richer. What did he do? He sent the acquaintance a bottle of Dom Pérignon and two very expensive gold-rimmed crystal glasses and a thank-you note. He didn't have to do that, but the recipient will never forget this guy.

4. *Keep your professional relationships professional.* If it looks like jealousy is rearing its ugly head, firmly but politely cut it off. When the relationship no longer serves you, no longer is mutually beneficial, step away from it. If the relationship you're building through networking appears to be harmful, take a sword to it.

5. *The key to networking is remembering the other person's need for achievement.* This is an important tip to keep in mind, especially when you're dealing with someone who's not as advanced in their career as you are. By respecting this need, providing guidance and leadership, sharing your personal experiences, this person will bring opportunities to you. Why? Because

the person values your insight, experience, and most of all the time and the knowledge you've shared. Acknowledge those who are on their way up. You may just find out one day that it was your extra effort that gave them the boost they needed.

So with your communication skills in place, you will increase your ability to work well with others. Listen, talk, share, sympathize, empathize. And when you extend your reach to work well with others that you know, you can extend your reach to work well with those you don't. You can develop networking skills and realize that networking is an incredible way to increase your opportunities tip by tip, contact by contact.

And now recall the laws of sowing and reaping, of giving and receiving. The more you give of yourself to communicate well with others and work well with others—the more you give—the more you'll receive as you strive to build your ambition.

6. *Learning to work with others who deserve it* is the last but most important key to working well with others. There is a distinction to this key—learn to work with others who *deserve* it, not those who *need* it. You must follow the guidelines of life itself. Life responds to those who work hard to achieve, so work with the people who deserve your assistance. In fact, you may have to show people how to deserve it—how to deserve your work, how to deserve your time, how to deserve your attention. Show people how to make small steps of progress, and reward them along the way. Show them how to deserve it one step at a time until finally they work themselves out of *need* and into *deserve*, out of the shadows of despair and poverty and into the light and power of ambition.

7

PRINCIPLE 6: SELF-APPRECIATION

Self-appreciation is the sixth step to building your ambition. Self-appreciation says, "Acknowledge your accomplishment; appreciate your potential." Know that your appreciation of yourself and your achievements will continually fuel the fire of ambition.

Self-appreciation is an integral part of success. You must develop a strong appreciation for your own style, your own methods, and your own process. There is no stereotype or model for success. There is no such thing. So, what exactly is success?

Success Is...

Success is the steady progress toward achieving your personal goals—designed by you, not by the latest No. 1 bestselling book, not by some philosophy imposed on you. Success is the steady progress toward achieving your own personal goals. Success is not a certain amount of money in your bank account. Success is being the person you want to be, having the things you want to have for yourself and for your family, your business goals, your personal goals, spiritual goals, health goals, the goals that give you satisfaction and joy.

To me, that's what success is. My definition of success could be radically different from yours. There's no one definition of success. In my personal opinion, self-centered material things have nothing to do with success. Success is your own steady progress toward the goals you set daily, weekly, monthly for your life, business, family—for yourself.

If someone tells me, "Hey, I'm cashing it all in and going to head for the mountains and live in a cabin and feed the squirrels and live off the land," and I hear later that this person did just that, I'd say this person was a smashing success. There is no one set way to be successful; there is only your way.

There is no one set way to be successful; there is only your way.

Success takes a combination of philosophies and ideologies—a combination of thoughts—to mold and to merge with your own. We need the mental food that others provide. We need mental exercise. We need to open our minds to a variety of alternatives. We need to learn to appreciate the other side of the debate so we can strengthen our own and defend our own. We need to expose ourselves to a wide range of thoughts, and listen to a variety of speakers, and read a variety of books. No one person or one speaker or one book has all the answers for you. We need a variety of influences to give us input, ideas, to manage our business, relationships, finances, to help us take advantage of our time. We need a variety of books in our library and tapes in our video and audio libraries. We need a variety of voices.

And here's what else we need—a variety of points of view, which can be so valuable. Somebody says, "Did you ever see it from over here?" And you say, "No." So you step over there where they are, and you take a look from their point of view, and you say, "My gosh, I never thought from this perspective. It's so different. No wonder you think the way you do."

Be Eager to Learn

Here's a clue for achieving success: take advantage of all that's available in terms of mental food and mental exercise. Always be eager to learn, no matter how far along you are in the journey, no matter where you are in your success. Gather up as much knowledge as you can. And then what? Debate it. Put it all on the table and look at it. Dissect it. Turn it around and stare at it. Ask questions. Make statements. Don't take it for granted that one person has all the answers you're looking for. Take their knowledge, but don't take it as the only knowledge.

Make sure that what you finally do, the model you develop of strong appreciation for your own style, your own methods, and your own process for achievement is a product of your own conclusion. That's what's valuable, not to just do what someone says without debating it. Consider the source, and then do it your way. You can take an interest in what someone says, digest it, take notes on it, but then debate it. Look at it from all angles. Be a student, not a follower.

Building the power of your ambition is a process unique to each and every one of us. Gather all the knowledge that you can; then develop your approach as a product of your own conclusions— your own conclusions, not someone else's conclusions. Don't fall for other people's philosophies. They may not be right. As you collect knowledge, you must sort through it and find what's valuable. Then you can develop your own philosophy, which becomes the most important of your guiding systems, one of your guiding lights.

Develop your own plan, lest you get into trouble with someone else's. Debate other people's plans, philosophies, achievement styles, the way they appreciate themselves. Debate all that. Why? Because it affects everything. The value you place on your plan, the value you place on yourself, the value you place on life in general affects everything around you. It even affects how you respect time—the 24 hours a day given to each of us to do with as we please. There's a connection between appreciating yourself and appreciating and respecting time. People who appreciate themselves understand and respect the use of time.

Time Management

The following is what I call the best kept secret of the rich. It is from an interesting discovery I made one day when I realized that rich people have 24 hours every day and poor people have 24 hours every day too. Wouldn't that drive you mad until you found out what the difference was? The difference between the two groups of people is the management of the time. A few simple disciplines practiced every day, and your whole life can change— your future can change; your income can change. But the rest of it is getting a handle on managing your time.

Chapter 4 focused on self-discipline. And now discipline shows up again here in the self-appreciation chapter, as self-discipline encompasses all aspects of a successful life. Discipline is important in how you manage the 24 hours given to you every day. So I want to give you a few tips to help you get a handle on the management of time.

1. Ignore the subject of time management. That's not a bad suggestion. Someone may say, "Well, I've been behind all my life. Doesn't look like that's going to change." I like that approach—at least it's honest. Nobody's ideas of success and time management are right for you unless they can be applied by you. We've already said that it's important to resist all stereotypes for success, to resist all models of success. So here's one alternative to time management: ignore the subject.

Don't let somebody pressure you by saying, "Here's what you have to do with your time." Resist all that. Take advice, but don't take orders. You can listen to their opinions, but then accept the ones you want to accept and forget the rest. Resist all attempts to pressure you into becoming someone else's model of success. Do it on your own time—the time that's right for you.

2. Another alternative to time management is to step down to an easier task—something more manageable, something that doesn't require as much time or effort. That's an alternative. Some people in sales are promoted to being manager and say, "Oh, now I have to be a manager. Heck with this! It takes 14 hours a day worrying about everybody. I'm going back out in the field, getting my sales job back." And that's a good alternative. Other people work for a company and say, "Oh, I'd love to own one of these franchises." Then they find out what it takes to own one and the kind of pressure and crazy number of hours. They can't play golf three days a week, so they finally say, "Hey, I've had it up to here with all the headaches, and drama, and dealing with all these people's lives, and running a company, and being responsible for all the stuff. I'm going to step down." And that's a good alternative. It really is.

Don't let yourself be pressured when stepping down might give you a better lifestyle. Case in point: A little girl complained that her father never played with her. She said, "Daddy comes home with his briefcase full of papers. He says "hello" to me, pats me on my head, and disappears. How come Daddy can't play with me when he comes home?" And her mother explained, "Your daddy works very hard. He loves you very much. But at the office, he's got so much to do that he can't get it all done. So he has to bring the rest of it home. That's why your daddy can't play with you." And the little girl says, "Why don't they just put him in a slower group?"

Not a bad idea. And I offer that here. If you're too busy to play with your kids, you need to join a slower group. You have to have time for your family. I went for some things that cost me too much in the early days. If I knew how much it was going to cost, I never would have paid the price. You have to weigh the consequences and determine how to make everything fit. Sometimes the extra money isn't worth it if it pressures you into losing touch with somebody you really care about. Family must be considered.

3. The best time management alternative is to get more out of you. If we just get more from ourselves, we can make an hour as valuable as ten hours used to be. We can get as much done now in a day as we used to get done in a week. Efficiency, skills, knowledge, awareness, practice, getting better—all of that value we can bring to the marketplace and the job, and that's where the real time management comes in.

A normal workday is enough time to get things accomplished. Eight to ten hours, five or six days a week, is a good amount of time—enough time. Many people today work from home. Their work is comprised mostly via the Internet so they can live wherever they want, not necessarily near their company headquarters. Guess what some of these folks found out? The projects that used to take two days can be completed in a few hours. Why? Because there are no distractions, no people stopping by their office to chat, no unsolicited phone calls to take, no unexpected visitors to deal with. When they work, they work. When they play, they play.

Not everyone has the luxury of a job like that, but some of the same principles can be applied at the office—like "do not disturb times" so you can work totally undisturbed during the hours when you do your best work; like setting certain hours each day to take appointments and phone calls. And that's really where the magic of personal development comes in: knowing who you are; becoming more valuable; being more valuable; knowing the value of your rhythms in completing certain tasks; getting things done more efficiently in a shorter period of time; working smarter, not harder.

Consider...

The following is a list of statements to consider regarding time management.

You run the day or it runs you.

Part of the key to time management is just staying in charge. But here's what usually happens: We start something and we're in control. But as time starts to unfold, we start losing control. You start a business and you're running it; yet soon it's running you. You have to stop every once in a while and say, "Hold it, hold it. Who's in charge here?" So here's a good phrase to jot down:

something masters, and something serves. That's the nature of life.

You have to make sure you are and will remain the master. You're the one in charge. Now here's how you can stay in charge: Have your written set of goals with you at all times. Then prioritize your goals according to importance. Constantly review your goals, matching up each one to a good written game plan—the game plan we talked about in Chapter 4, the game plan that says, "Take it out of your head and put it down on paper." Then with your game plan in hand, try to separate the majors from the minors—the really important things from the things you just have to do. And prioritize: Is this a major day or a minor day? Adjust your time accordingly. Is this a major conversation or a minor conversation? Don't major in minor things. Don't spend too much time on things that don't count and too little time on things that should count. So you're about to pick up the phone and make a call. But before you do, decide: Is this a major call or is this a minor call? If it's a major call, it needs a little preparation. If it's a minor call, a few pleasantries will probably do. "Hi. How are you?" Tell a little joke. Exchange some pleasantries. So a little evaluation will save you a lot of time—major, minor.

Don't mistake movement for achievement.

You probably know people who just play at being busy, thinking they have to be busy being productive. It's easy to get faked out by being busy. How many people come home after work at night and flop down in the easy chair and say, "I was going, going, going all day"? Very many, I venture to say. But the real question is, going where and doing what? Some people are going, going, going, doing figure eights. They're not making much progress. Don't mistake movement for achievement. Evaluate the hours in your days and see if there's not a lot of wasted time that you could manage better, do more with.

Good time management means concentration and focus.

You have to zero in on the job at hand, concentrate. Don't start your business day until you get to the business. I used to start my business day in the shower, trying to compose a letter in the shower although the cobwebs haven't been cleared out yet and I'm not fully awake. It doesn't work. Wait until you get to your workplace to start your work. Don't start your business day at the breakfast table. It's not good for the family, and you really can't give the work the focus required.

Don't think about work on the way to work. If you drive to work, focus on driving, not the conference call coming up. There are a lot of cars on the highway. Can you imagine if everybody driving to work was thinking about work? There would be accidents everywhere. On the way to work, concentrate on the drive. In the shower, concentrate on getting clean. At the breakfast table, concentrate on the family. Wherever you are, be there. Don't be somewhere else in your mind. Give whatever you're doing the gift of attention. Give people the gift of attention. The gift of attention, concentration, and focus leads to good time management.

Another time management essential: *learn to say "no."* It's easy in a social society to say, "Yes, yes, yes" too much and over-obligate yourself. Don't say "yes" too quickly. Better to say you don't know if you can make it and you'll give a call. Better to say you don't know than to later back out. One of my colleagues has a good saying: "Don't let your mouth overload your back." Committing too soon, too quickly, being too eager to please and be nice will backfire. Appreciate yourself, your time, and your time limits.

Self-appreciation includes special time alone and with those you love and who love you.

This is especially important for charity and volunteer work time as well. A group of entrepreneurs I know have been very successful in their business; consequently, they receive a lot of press that generates numerous requests to do pro bono work. They handle the demand by weighing each of the requests in regard to time commitment, evaluate for opportunities, then take a collective vote on which two to accept during the next 12 months.

Don't immediately say "yes" to offers that sound prestigious or social functions or events that sound like a lot of fun. Say "maybe," and take time to evaluate what's an important contribution to your career or society and what will take time away from your ambitions and your family. Be eager to please yourself and your family. Don't be so eager to please everybody else. Appreciate your own limits. You don't have to fill up every second of the day. Take time to appreciate what you've accomplished. Your success should be a pleasure. Appreciating what you have and what you've done and who you've become is important. It's an important component in fueling your future achievements.

Self-appreciation is acknowledging your game-plan accomplishments.

Knowing you finished all you started out to do that day is encouraging. Daily gains continue to fuel your achievement. Let's say you're figuring out tomorrow's game plan tonight, and tomorrow looks pretty light. So all you write down for tomorrow is "Cleanup Day." Take time to take care of all the little notes on your desk. Write the thank-you notes you've been meaning to write all week. Take care of a few phone calls that keep getting shuffled from one day to the next—nothing major, just minor stuff. Nonetheless, little stuff will keep nagging on you until you get it done. Just do it, and at the end of the day you will feel you've accomplished a lot.

Minor achievements are just as important as major achievements. Why? Because you can't appreciate the big achievements without first appreciating the little ones. Success is the constant process of working toward your goals.

Enjoy the plateau.

George Leonard, in his book *Mastery*, talks about enjoying the plateau, which is an important point in self-appreciation and time management. So often we race to get ahead, thinking about our next achievement so much that we can't appreciate the time in between. Happiness is not in the getting; happiness is in the becoming. Happiness is a universal quest. Happiness is a joy that mostly comes as a result of positive activity. It has a wide variety of meanings, a wide variety of interpretations. Happiness is both the joy of discovery and the joy of knowing. It's the result of an awareness of the full range of life, experiences, sounds, harmonies, dreams, goals, and the joy that comes from designing a life that practices the fine art of living well.

Happiness is exploring all that life offers and quite often found in having options—options of doing what you *want* to instead of doing what you *have* to; the option of living where you want to instead of living where you have to; the option of looking like you want to instead of settling for what you have to. Happiness is receiving and sharing, reaping and bestowing. Happiness is found in taking time to enjoy what you've accomplished, in enjoying the plateau, in giving yourself credit when credit is due, in patting yourself on the back for a job well done.

Happiness is not in the getting; happiness is in the becoming.

Happiness is here and now—not the end result. Happiness is part of the journey. There's an old saying that goes, "The road to heaven is heaven." The happiness that you're searching for in the future must be found today. The success you're after in the future will only be found by working on it today.

Self-Appreciation Reflection and Inventory

Success is the balance between the need for active achievement and the satisfaction in taking the time to acknowledge what you've already achieved. Take time to reflect while you're enjoying the plateau. And while you're reflecting on your past accomplishments, think about something else—the potential within you that's still untapped.

Consider these questions during your time of reflection:

- What could I have achieved in the past had I been more diligent?

- Could I have been more disciplined?

- Worked smarter instead of harder?

- Said "no" more often to social functions, to community commitments?

- What could I have achieved in the past had I tried something different?

Only you can answer these questions that are very personal. While you're reflecting and enjoying your plateau, I ask that you dig a little deeper and see if you can't be a bit more effective next time—work a little smarter instead of a little harder. So, that's the number one question: What could I have achieved in the past if I tried a little more diligently?

How can I achieve more in the future?

If you have taken quality time to thoughtfully answer question number one, you'll probably have a clue as to what's needed in the future. Do you need to work more diligently? Do you need to be more disciplined? Do you need to work smarter instead of harder? Do you need to say "no" more often? Do you need to manage your time better? That's one of the keys to reflection. Put down on paper what worked for you in the past and figure out ways to translate this information into the future. You can design your better future if you can learn from your past. You can face your future with more excitement and more anticipation when you design a future worth getting excited about.

You can see your future and have it pull you toward it. But don't forget to appreciate yourself for what you have done so far, for what you have done today. Take a self-appreciation inventory. Ask yourself a few questions: What have I achieved in the last four days, the last two weeks, the last six months, the last year, the last ten years? What have I achieved during these time periods? Write it down.

Take an honest inventory of yourself.

Take a self-appreciation inventory of all you've done, and all you've accomplished, and all you've become. Take inventory of yourself. Now compare this list to your goals. Have you accomplished all you set out to do in the last four days, two weeks, six months, one year, ten years? Compare your list. Maybe you've been so busy trying to reach your goals that you haven't taken the time to sit back and reflect on where you've really been.

Now you can look back at your list and say, "Wow, I really have been through a lot. I really have learned a lot. Look what I've done. Look what I've become. I wasn't like this ten years ago or even one year ago. Look at me. I'm doing okay." Building your ambition takes little steps—one step at a time, one day at a time, one week at a time.

It's like taking your family to a reunion where people haven't seen your kids for six months or even a year. They say, "My, look how you've grown." You know your kids have grown, but when you see them every day, it's hard to notice. It's the same way when considering your personal growth. So write down all your accomplishments and see where you've been and what you've done and who you've become. You'll say, "Oh, look how I've grown!"

What could I have achieved that I didn't?

Be honest now. This is your inventory. Nobody else has to see it. What could you have achieved over the last week, the last month, the last quarter, the last year, what could you have achieved that you didn't? Would a game plan have made a difference? Would your direction have made a difference? Would greater preparation have made a difference? Would more discipline have made a difference in how you changed your habits, changed your life? Would time management have made a difference—major time over minor time? Ask yourself, "What could I have achieved that I didn't?"

Now take this one step further: "What do I want to achieve in the next four days, the next two weeks, the next six months, over the next year, over the next ten years? What do I want to achieve?" All of this falls in line with your goals. What you *could* achieve has to fall in line with what you *want* to achieve. What you *could* do has to line up with what you *want* to do. And what you *could* become has to meet "what do I *want* to become?" Everything affects everything. And through the proper disciplines practiced every day, the "what *could* I do?" has to match up with "what do I *want* to do?"

What can I do to achieve this goal that I'm not doing now?

"What things do I need to work on that I'm not working on now?" Remember, it's easy to do the disciplines, the little things every day—and it's easy not to do the disciplines every day. Look back at the self-knowledge inventory you took in Chapter 2: "Self-Direction." Look back at the list you made of your three most important work-related goals. Look back at your list of the three most important personal and spiritual goals. How are you doing with these? Are you making a little progress each day? Are you appreciative of the progress you've made so far? It's important that you take time out to acknowledge yourself, your achievements, what you've done so far, where you've come, who you've become.

Self-appreciation is a stage in building the power of ambition that takes a little more maturity, a greater resolve, knowing that you'll do it until you get it done. Take the time to acknowledge yourself for doing it. Self-appreciation comes from already being firmly set on the course of positive self-direction, being on the right track, having that wonderful blend of humility and self-esteem, knowing within yourself that you're accomplishing your goals, and knowing yourself enough and being confident in yourself enough to avoid needless bragging.

Self-appreciation says that you admit there's room for improvement—knowing you're on the right track but admitting the need for continued growth by reading more books, attending more seminars, learning more skills, following more disciplines, having a greater awareness and bigger vision. There's always more room to grow and more knowledge to gain.

Being knowledgeable is an important part of the path to wealth and good health. We must never stop learning, growing, expanding—and never forget to take time to appreciate ourselves for what we've done in pursuit of what we want to become.

8

BALANCE

So far in this book we have discussed and examined the six principles of building the power of our ambition. Before we go into how ambition affects our personal lives, let's briefly review those principles.

1. **Self-direction:** knowing who you are and where you want to go with your life.

2. **Self-reliance:** taking responsibility for your own life and taking responsibility for all that happens in your life.

3. **Self-discipline:** addressing ambition at the daily level; doing all you can every day and doing it until you get there; knowing that the pain of discipline weighs ounces and the pain of regret weighs tons.

4. **Self-enterprise:** keeping your eyes and ears open at all times; being aware of opportunities around you and creating opportunities that keep you on the road to success.

5. **Working with others:** learning how to effectively communicate with those around you; learning how to maximize your networking abilities; and learning to work with those who deserve it, not those who need it.

6. **Self-appreciation:** fueling your accomplishments tomorrow by acknowledging your successes today.

Each of these six building blocks works together in creating and directing energy to fuel our ambitions.

As we look now at ambition and how it affects our personal life, remember the building blocks already discussed. Balancing your personal life with your professional life is key to making ambition work for you. Home life and work life must work together, ensuring that what you're going for in your career complements your home life and what goes on at home complements your career. One won't work well if the other doesn't.

For example, a woman arrives at work early in the morning and is the last one to leave every night. This routine continues week after week, month after month, yet she doesn't accomplish any more than anyone else. It seems she's using the office to escape from home. Something's wrong that needs to be fixed. Chances are that whatever's bothering her at home is affecting her work. Her work life and home life are off balance.

Home life and work life must work together to be successful.

Another example: A man is always late for work and regularly takes off during the middle of the day to go home to tend to some sort of emergency. He also takes long breaks, and his work is faltering. It seems the "emergencies" at home are excuses to stay away from the job.

If something's wrong at work, fix it if you can or look for your solution elsewhere. If something's wrong at home, fix it. If what's going on at home is the result of neglect, admit it and fix it. Pay greater attention to balancing work and home life. If you need to go to counseling, go to counseling. Talk with your minister, talk with a trusted friend. Remember that whatever the problem is at home, it probably didn't happen overnight. So make sure to give it time to heal; be patient.

Find a Healthy Balance

For a healthy life, there must be balance between work time and home time, professional time and personal time. Both have to be working well to maximize your ambition and your potential. Problems at home affect work. Problems at work affect home. Even when things are going well in both areas, sometimes special circumstances call for work to take away from home time. When that's the case, make sure everybody at home knows when to expect the light at the end of the tunnel. And if the extra project is taking significant time away from the family, make sure your family knows that their time will be paid back with interest.

Psychologists have discovered what brings humans the most happiness and satisfaction:

1. **Our work and our contribution to society;** continued progress toward reaching our goals and activity that generates our lifestyle, influence, power.

2. **Love.** The love we receive from our spouse, our children, our parents, our families, our friends. Knowing

that one person or several people care about us, want to spend time with us.

The professional goals you have outlined for yourself take a lot of work, discipline, and skills. They include constant learning to improve and develop yourself and your skills. Don't expect your achievements to come to you on a silver platter. Are you working on the wish and the hope and the prayer philosophy? Don't—you're wasting your time. Your goals require constant attention and discipline every day or they will never come to you at all.

Maintaining a healthy personal and family life takes as much attention as creating the perfect professional life.

157

You can't just come home at night after work, after a long day, and expect that your family life is growing just fine all by itself. You can't just expect that your personal life will grow and flourish without attention, without taking time to feed and water and weed out the bad stuff, the negative stuff that happens while you're away. No, creating the perfect personal and family life takes just as much attention as creating the perfect professional life. It takes love and nurturing and kindness and sincerity and caring.

Unfortunately, people spend all their time, focus all their energy, and give everything they have to the job. It won't work that way. Your family deserves more than your leftover time. The investment we make in our personal relationships before they're put on paper is the investment we must continue to make. The more we give, the more we get. If you stop giving, guess what? You'll probably stop receiving too. So keep your investment in relationships and family active and balanced. That's part of the good life.

What good is a mansion on the hill if you have no one to share it with? It's no good. What good is an investment portfolio worth millions if you have no one to share it with? It's no good. What good is working so hard day after day, month after month, year after year—working, working, working until you accumulate everything you want—and in the meantime, your family left you? It's no good. It all loses its value.

Life has to be balanced: Work hard; play hard. Work six days; take one day off. Work three months; take one week off. That is not balance. Life has to be balanced or your lifestyle will suffer. Life without balance can cost your relationships. Life without balance can cost your health. Life without balance can cost your spirituality. Life without balance can cost your wealth. Balance brings happiness. Work on balancing your work and family life. Work on balancing your ambitions with the lifestyle you desire.

If you're a believer, don't neglect your spiritual life. Putting off your faith quickly infects your whole being and becomes a disease. I'm not asking you to be a believer, but I am asking that if you are a believer, don't neglect that part of your future success. Study and put your faith into practice as diligently as you study and practice ambition, and parenting, and skills, and success in the marketplace. Faith helps sustain ambition.

A healthy, balanced body is the best support system you will ever have.

Another important aspect in building your power of ambition is your physical side—the health of your body and well-being. The best advice I have regarding our physical wellness comes from an ancient scripture that says we are to treat our body like a temple.

Excellent advice. Treating our body like a temple means taking extremely good care of it. A temple is not a woodshed. A temple is full of valuable treasures—as is our body, comprised of our brain, heart, digestive system, muscles, and so many other vital parts that keep us alive and in good health.

Our body is built on balance to function well. Our body needs to be a good support system for our mind and the spirit—a good support system that can take us where we want to go and support us with strength, and energy, and power, and vitality. I believe that vitality is a major part of success. I've witnessed that some people don't do well simply because they don't feel well. Feeling well is a personal responsibility addressed by taking care of the temple. Your physical body is the only place you have to live—cherish it.

Ancient scripture says that "sometimes the spirit is willing, but the body is weak." That's a sad combination—a willing spirit and a weak body. I can't think of a much more pitiful combination. You wake up in the morning and the mind says, "Let's get busy and make this the most productive day so far!" And the body says, "I can't even get out of bed." You must now have a serious conversation with your body: "That's the last time you're going to fail me. Give me another excuse that you can't get out of bed and I'll drive you to your knees to do push-ups until you're exhausted. I have plans for fortune and enterprise, and I demand a strong, unbelievably powerful support system. From now on, I'm going to have a support system that will take me wherever I want to go. Support me with power; support me with vitality, strength, uniqueness, zest. Anything less than that, I will not settle for."

You have to take care of the physical side of yourself because it's so important to your overall health. Be conscious of your support system. Be conscious of yourself but not so self-conscious that you jog or lift weights six hours a day. Spending 20 to 30 minutes every day walking or exercising can give you a strong, healthy body. You can work in extra exercise every day doing just a few simple things like walking up a few flights of stairs instead of taking the elevator. When looking for a parking space, park where you have to walk a bit.

The best exercise routine in the world is the one that you'll do.

I have found that the best exercise program in the world is the one that works for you, the one you'll do, the program that won't bore you or hurt you. If you don't like to jog, if your joints can't handle it, go for a walk. If you don't like to walk, take up swimming half a mile a few times a week. If you don't like exercise that seems like exercise, get into a sport like tennis, or racquetball, or basketball, or softball. You don't have to do too much—just enough to keep your body moving.

When you participate in a regular exercise program, you will feel better—not just your body, but your mind will feel better too! It is somewhat of a paradox in that the more physical activity, the less sleep you need. The more physical activity, the better your mind works. Perhaps you have heard of the "runner's high." It's true. After 20 to 30 minutes of sustained activity, endorphins are released into our bloodstream. Endorphins are our body's natural secretion of morphine.

When you take care of your physical being, your entire well-being is healthier and happier. You will have the muscle strength and the vitality to take you wherever you want to go, accomplish whatever you want to accomplish. Develop a good physical support system to take care of yourself and make all of your dreams come true.

Balance in All Things

It is wise to pay attention to what can get out of balance and affect your ambition, such as overeating, smoking, drugs, and drinking too much alcohol. These things can destroy your temple just as surely as pure neglect. A fine glass of wine with dinner may be one of your joys, but drinking too much, too often will tear down your temple. And drinking too much at business dinners or social events will alienate you from the professionals who know their limits. Pay attention to your behavior in the marketplace lest it cost you more than you'd like to pay. It's all about balance.

How does your ambition in the marketplace translate into a balanced life at home? If you're giving too much at work, pay it back to your family with a movie night or special outing. Balance is important. If you don't have balance, you may be sacrificing your family for your work, being careful with your clients and careless with your children. Without balance, there's a price to pay that can cost us all that is the most precious to us in life—our loved ones. So evaluate the price before you begin setting and reaching your goal. *What must I give up to achieve this goal? What must I become?* Evaluate it all, each aspect.

Do you think your disciplines at work can affect your personal life? Do you think the skills you perfect at work affect your personal life? Of course. The skills you bring from work have an enormous bearing on your personal life. All disciplines affect each other. Nothing stands alone. Everything affects everything. Everything matters. Yes, some things don't matter as much, but there isn't anything that doesn't matter—nothing at all. Don't be casual in your approach to life and business and family. How you treat your children will undoubtedly affect how you treat your clients. How you run your office will undoubtedly affect how you run your life, your home. Everything matters.

Leadership

Now let's look at leadership. The skills of leadership are required at work, yes; but they're also required at home with our families and the community. I call leadership the challenge to be something more than mediocre—a step up to the new challenge, the new opportunity. It is said of Abraham Lincoln that he was at his mother's bedside when she died. Her last words were "Be somebody, Abe." And if that story is true, evidently he took it to heart and proceeded from that moment to become somebody.

When it comes to being a leader, if you really want to attract quality people, the key is to become a person of quality. Leadership is the ability to attract someone to the gifts and skills and opportunities you offer as an owner, as a manager, as a parent. I call leadership the great challenge of life, in a wide variety of areas including science and politics, industry and education, sales, etc. But the greatest leadership challenge is parenting. Leadership is not just getting our salespeople or business colleagues ready for the next century; it's getting our children ready for the future.

If you really want to attract quality people, the key is to become a person of quality.

Refined and Effective

All great leadership keeps working on itself until it becomes refined and effective. Refinement means a lot of things, including learning to be *strong but not rude*. Becoming a powerful, capable leader with a wide range of reach includes being strong. Some people mistake rudeness for strength. It's not even a good substitute.

Refinement also means being *kind but not weak.* We must not mistake weakness for kindness. Kindness isn't weak. Kindness is a certain type of strength. We must be kind enough to tell somebody the truth. We must be kind and considerate enough to lay it on the line, to tell it like it is—not deal in delusion.

Next, learn to be *bold but not a bully.* It takes boldness to win the day to fulfill your ambitions. You have to stride out front. You have to be willing to take the first arrow, the first problem, the first trouble. I think you would agree that farming is not an easy job. Farmers face weeds, rains, and bugs straight on. But to reap any value at harvest, farmers—like you and me—have to meet every challenge and bring home the harvest.

Leadership refinement also means to be *humble but not timid.* You can't get to the high life by being timid. Some people mistake timidity for humility, but humility is a virtue; timidity is a disease, an affliction. It can be cured, but it's a problem. Humility is a God-like word evoking a sense of awe, a sense of wonder and awareness of the human soul and spirit—something unique about the human drama versus the rest of life. Humility is a grasp of the distance between us and the stars yet having the feeling that we're part of the stars.

Refinement is to be *proud but not arrogant.* It takes pride to win the day and build your ambition. It takes pride in community, in cause, in accomplishment—but the key is to be proud without being arrogant. The worst kind of arrogance is arrogance from ignorance, which is intolerable and can be expensive.

Refinement is *humor without folly.* A good sense of humor is important for a leader, but not folly. Leaders can be witty but not silly, fun but not foolish.

Leadership refinement is learning how to *deal in realities and truth.* Life is unique; accept it as unique. Some people call it tragic, but I think the whole drama of life is unique, fascinating. Likewise, leadership is unique. The skills that work well for one leader may not work at all for another, but the fundamental skills of leadership can probably be massaged a bit to work well for just about everyone at work, in the community, at home.

Raising a Balanced Family

Many people assume that the skills involved in having a good, solid family come naturally. To whom? Most schools don't teach How to Raise a Family 101 or How to Raise a Family 102. They don't. They should, but they don't. People tend to assume that good leaders in the community are automatically good leaders at home. Some are, and some aren't.

Communication

What are some necessary skills when raising a good, solid family? *Communication* is number one. Every member of the family has to know they have a voice, and that their voice is respected, and that their opinions count. The family is a democracy, so if there's an issue, they can put it on the table. The dinner table is not just a place for the evening meal. No, it's a place to bring out all the issues, to talk about the day, share experiences, ask questions, and hope for answers—around the dinner table.

In today's society, there are a lot of broken homes, divorced parents who share custody of the children. How do you raise good, solid kids when they're split between two households? Make sure the philosophies in both households are compatible. Obviously the reigning philosophies are different; that's why the home is split. But if you are a parent facing this kind of challenge, put away the personal differences and develop one set of philosophies by which to raise the kids. Why? If you don't, the kids will be a mess. If there is one set of rules for one house and another set of rules in the other house, the children will grow up confused and left wondering what's right and what's wrong.

Regardless of how your household is set up, make sure there is open and honest communication. Everybody needs a voice. Everybody has to be heard. And everybody has to acknowledge that everyone else's voice counts. That's number one: communication.

Activity

Raising a solid, balanced family includes *activity*. A study done a while back surveyed a large group of happy families. What they all had in common: first, they had a regular habit of eating dinner together as often as possible; second, they were all involved in a physical activity like walks, tennis, swimming, basketball—they planned family physical fitness activities; third, they made a regular habit of spending Sunday mornings in church; and fourth, the parents scheduled quality personal time together alone. Why would the parents' personal time affect the entire family so dramatically? Because when the parents are happy with each other and invest in each other, they present a unified front for the kids. Personal time together is important.

Raising a solid, balanced, happy family includes planned activities together. Bike rides in the summer; ski trips in the winter; boating, fishing, trips to the zoo, frisbee in the yard, baseball, softball, basketball—whatever interests your family has, make sure you take time to schedule these kinds of outside activities on a regular basis. Scheduled inside activities are important as well—doing things together at home on a regular basis. If you have a young family used to plopping down in front of the TV during every spare moment, start weaning them off this habit one day a week. Plan one evening a week without the TV. During this time, read together, work on household projects together, go through the family picture albums and videos together. Plan vacations together. Even clean the house together. Being together is the key.

Being together is the key.

Start a family journal; write in it once a week: what all you did, where all you went, and what all you saw, and how all you felt. Family journals are a wonderful way of tracking the growth of your family and the growth of your kids. When you look back on these family journals, you'll find they're one of the greatest treasures you have. And here's another fun way to log the history of your family. A friend of mine tells that when she was a kid, one of three in a family where sibling rivalry was at its height, her parents used to hide a tape recorder under the dining room table every so often and tape the family dinner conversation. Wow. Those kids get together now and have a great time with this stuff. They're grown now, but when they look back and listen to their upbringing, it has a way of rekindling the family bond.

Spiritual Connection

The third most important key to raising a strong, healthy family with bonds that will last a lifetime is a *spiritual connection.* I know your beliefs are your own, and whether or not you call the power behind our existence God or not is entirely up to you. But whatever your faith is, whatever your beliefs are, share them with your family. Share them with your children. Make time frequently to discuss the spiritual aspects of life. Give your kids the opportunity of choice by giving them a basis of knowledge. There are all sorts of wonderful and valuable programs that churches provide these days in addition to the Sunday sermon. There is Sunday school for kids, vacation Bible school, camping trips, family outings, weekly Bible studies, picnics, plays, musicals, concerts, and special interest groups. If you're searching for a church home, visit several churches to see which is right for you and your family.

A Balanced Lifestyle

There are many ways to build strong bonds and healthy relationships with your family. The tips I gave you are just a few. You may have other great ideas. Just remember that the more energy, time, and attention you give to your family, the more love and attention you'll receive in return.

Your children will love you unconditionally when they're young—just make sure that as they mature, you've given them a reason to continue their unconditional love. Be with your family at home and outdoors. Go to church together. Talk with each other. Get to know your children—who they are; what their dreams are, their visions of the future. You will never be sorry for taking time for them. Your children are not just miniature versions of you. They're special little people with their own personalities.

The greatest satisfaction after a productive day's work is coming home to a harmonious family. Balance between work and home is part of a healthy and happy lifestyle. It's where ambition can lead you—if you deem it part of your course.

9

AMBITION
ECONOMICS

The economics of ambition, the rewards of ambition, the final result of working hard, burning the midnight oil, "doing it until," being disciplined to stay on track day after day, week after week, month after month—what's all this hard work going to get you? Better put, what's all this working *smart* going to get you?

If you put into practice what you have read in the first eight chapters of this book about the power of ambition, as you set your goals and developed a game plan and used the tools of reflection and discipline when putting your life together to reach your destination, surely somewhere in all your writings you wrote down *wealth.*

I'm sure you didn't write down that you wanted to earn enough to just get by. No, you probably wrote down that you wanted to have a certain amount of money. To some, it may be to earn $50,000 a year. To others, it may be to earn $500,000 a year, or a million dollars. It doesn't matter. You probably wrote down what you believe you're capable of earning if you really exercised your potential, what you want to earn next year, three years, five years, ten years from now—and even have a total in mind to have earned over your lifetime.

That figure probably would be viewed by the majority as being rich, getting the most from your ambition, being rewarded by your ambition. I'm not talking about the incredible feelings of accomplishment. Now we are discussing the tangible rewards of ambition. How wealthy should you be in knowledge and in spirit? As wealthy as you possibly can be. How rich should you be in dollars and investments? As rich as you possibly can be. I'm not talking greed. I'm talking reward for success at the service of others, not at the expense of others.

Is it okay to strive for success? Is it okay to strive to become rich and wealthy? Many people struggle with the concept of being rich. Rich people seem to lack morals. Rich people are cutthroat. Rich people don't care. No, that's not true. Of course some rich people lack morals, are cutthroat, and don't care, but a lot of poor people have those same traits. So corruption is not inherent with being rich or wealthy; corruption is inherent with gaining at the expense of others. Corruption is evil, but wealth is not evil. Wealth says, "Discover your own talents and use them and take care of them so your talents and skills and gifts can take care of you."

It's our natural destiny to grow, succeed, prosper, and find happiness.

The more I ponder this topic of wealth, I firmly believe that it's our natural destiny to grow, to succeed, to prosper, and to find happiness. So here's what I've learned to do to temper the words *rich* and *wealthy*. I call it becoming "financially independent." Financial independence is the ability to live from the income of your own personal resources. That's a little easier for some to swallow than rich or wealthy, because they have the mistaken idea that to be wealthy or rich you have to misuse people, tell lies, and throw away values. If being rich bothers you, don't pursue riches.

Some people even tell me that the Bible says it's hard for a rich person to reach heaven. I say, "Well, that language suits me. It didn't say it was impossible; it just said it was hard. I don't mind a little hard stuff." I'm also reminded that the Bible says, "The meek shall inherit the earth." But where does it say that to be meek you have to be poor? No, the Bible doesn't say you have to be poor. That's just an interpretation, a poor rationalization that lazy people use—people who need to justify their lack of progress, people who will give up in the midst of any adversity, people who don't even try.

Financial Independence

For everyone born in the United States or who comes to America, part of your heritage is the opportunity to become financially independent. In a nation that's full of hope and promise, it's our heritage and our right and within our reach to realize all the best that exists, including personal wealth.

One part of ambition economics is based on how you want to live. Some people need millions of dollars for all the projects they have going, all the causes they support. And that's what is exciting about the US—you can make it happen if you are determined. Are there books on the subject? Yes, of course. There's plenty of information on how to be rich. Other people lead modest lives. But no matter the financial goals, financial independence is every American's heritage—to someday become financially independent and live off the income of your own personal resources. Wow, that's freedom of the most exciting kind—financial independence.

To become as wealthy or rich or financially independent as you want to become, you first have to settle that for yourself: it's okay to be rich and wealthy, but it depends how you earn the money, of course. Success must be at the service of others, not at the expense of others. Everybody has to weigh this for themselves; I understand that.

Financial independence is the ability to live from the income of your own personal resources.

1. A Matter of Philosophy

Let's say that you'd like to go for becoming financially independent. First there is the matter of philosophy—the philosophy of the rich. Rich people invest their money and spend what's left. The difference in your economic future is not the economy; the difference in your economic future is your philosophy.

One time a lady chastised me severely, saying, "Mr. Rohn, you can't promise young people that they can become rich and wealthy, financially independent. It's just not in the cards these days. It takes everything a person makes just to keep their head above water and the wolf away from the door."

I said, "No, that's not true."

She said, "It *is* true. You can't hold out hope to all people who listen to you and read your books, telling them they can become financially independent, especially children. They'll be sadly disillusioned. It's not in the cards these days."

I said, "Gosh, I wish I could persuade you otherwise. Let me use this illustration. Can you think of a couple right now who makes $5,000 a month?"

She said, "Yes. If I think real hard, I could come up with a couple who makes $5,000 a month."

"What would they tell you it takes just to keep their head above water and the wolf away from the door?"

"They would probably say, 'All of it. It takes $5,000 a month.'"

I said, "Can you think of a couple who makes $5,500?"

She said, "Yes, I probably can."

I said, "What would they tell you it takes just to keep their nose above water and the wolf away from the door?"

"They'd say, 'All of it.'"

I said, "Now if they said it took all of it, how do you account for the extra $500? There are errors in your judgment of economic philosophy. You say, 'No, Mr. Rohn, it's the economy.' I say, no, it's the philosophy. If the couple saved the $500 and lived like the other couple living on $5,000, the extra $500 a month invested over the next 15 years would make them financially independent. The difference is not your paycheck; the difference is your philosophy."

What to Do with a Dollar

So now let me teach you some of the best philosophy I know—what to do with a dollar.

After I persuade some kids that it's okay to become rich, powerful, and financially independent, I say, "Here's what you do with a dollar. To begin with, never spend more than 70 cents. And here's a good plan for the remaining 30 cents. First I suggest you take 10 cents out of every dollar and give it to charity."

Here's why I tell them that: nothing teaches kids character better than generosity. By supporting worthy projects, they learn that taking a piece of what they've been blessed with and giving it to help people who can't help themselves is what really matters in life. The time to start this good habit is when the amounts are small. When kids understand this concept, they will give a dime out of every dollar. It's easy to give a dime out of a dollar; it's a little tougher to give $100,000 out of $1 million.

Someone may say, "Oh, if I had a million, I'd give $100,000." I'm not so sure. That's a lot of money. It's better to start early with a little so you'll be ready when talking about big dollars.

So, 10 cents out of every dollar for charity. Then I tell the kids, "The other 10 cents of the 30 cents is active capital. Active capital is what you use to make a profit." I teach the kids if they have two bicycles, one is for them to ride and they can rent out the other. That's how I teach kids what an active capital fund is. Kids are happy to learn about this; after all, profits are better than wages. Kids need to know that. The benefits of living in a capitalistic society is that kids can start a lemonade stand before they can get a job. Kids can clean out their rooms, have a garage sale, and earn a profit.

Wages make you a living; profits make you a fortune.

In the United States, we live in a capitalistic society where the money belongs in the hands of the people, not in the hands of the government. So you should turn part of your wages into capital, into a profit-making enterprise. It can be a piece of property, anything. Buy, sell—it doesn't matter what it is; try to show a profit.

It doesn't take a kid long to figure out that profits are better than wages, better than allowances. And that's what America is all about—making a profit. And here's what's exciting: you can make a profit long before you can legitimately earn a wage. There are no limits. Your profits can sometimes accelerate much faster than your wages. Teach your kids early: profits are better than wages. Wages make you a living; profits make you a fortune.

I believe every American should try their hand at making a profit since we live in a capitalistic society. How long will it take to triple your wages currently? A while. But with profits, there's no limit. Once I understood this, I went bonkers. Profits benefit the whole world. I talked to a man who rents a lot of apartments. He said, "Mr. Rohn, you wouldn't believe it, but when most people leave an apartment, it's trashed."

I said, "You have to be kidding!"

He said, "No."

What a reputation to leave behind.

A friend of mine has made money on every car he's bought. Why? Because when he traded it in or sold it, it was always better than he found it.

The key for parents is to touch a life and leave it better than you found it. Touch a business and leave it better than you found it. Touch a job and leave it better than you found it. Whether you stay six weeks, six months, or six years, always leave it better than you found it. Make a contribution. Leave a profit. What a world this would be if everybody left a profit, not a piece of trash.

So, after spending no more than 70 cents of every dollar, there are 30 cents remaining. I teach the kids (and anyone who wants to be successful) that the first 10 cents go to charity, the second 10 cents go to active capital, and the third 10 cents are for passive capital—and you can become as wealthy as you want!

Passive capital is when you allow someone else to use some of your money. You're the passive partner, and the active partner tries to make a profit and then pay you interest. One of the most valuable aspects of this arrangement is called compound interest—nothing more valuable. I suggest 10 cents for passive capital. Let someone else use it, pay you interest on it.

Now here's what else I teach kids; it's a Bible philosophy, and here's what it says: "The borrower is servant to the lender." Excellent concept! If you've taught (or learned) this properly and then ask the kids, "What do you want to be?" they'll say, "I want to be one of those lenders." That's the power position. If you're interested in power for the future, influence for the future, and being ruler over much, the key is to be one of those lenders—not a spender, a lender.

Be a lender, not a spender.

If you can't reach this life-changing formula right now, start where you can and work toward it. The 70, 10, 10, and 10 is the ideal. It doesn't matter if you're trying to lose weight, improve your health, or get your finances in order, here's the key: set up the ideal and work toward it.

Keep Strict, Accurate Accounts

When building your financial independence, keep strict accounts. Don't let yourself or anyone else talk you out of keeping accurate, up-to-date accounts. You have to know exactly where your financial resources come from and where they go. Don't fall into the "I don't know where it all goes" trap. Don't fall into the "It just gets away from me" mindset. No. Keep strict records of all accounts, which is so easy with all the financial software readily available. It's as easy as entering your deposits and checks and receipts, and the computer program will tell you exactly where you stand.

And it does more than that. If you're really wondering where it all goes, the computer will tell you that too. Most of the programs let you categorize your expenditures, print it out, and you'll know exactly by category where it all goes. And when it's right there in front of you, you can evaluate what you're buying and what you're wasting. Take that wasting part and add it to one of your capital funds. It'll get you where you want to be that much faster.

2. A Matter of Attitude

And here's another important part of building your financial independence—your attitude. First is *philosophy about money.* Second is *attitude about money.* The best attitude foundation is to know that everyone must pay for democracy, free enterprise, marketplace, and a country second to none with gifts brought here from all around the world. I finally became a happy taxpayer after I was educated. You may say, "Well, the government misuses it." What do you care? That's not going to make any difference in your future, is it? If true, it's not going to greatly reduce your chances to become rich and powerful. It shouldn't make any difference at all whether taxes are misused or not.

Sure, we need to vote well so the country is run as well as possible and there's as level a playing field as possible. But what if there isn't? You can't base your life on that; instead, vote well, chart your own course, and take charge of your own life. We all have to pay. And after you pay your taxes, pay yourself first. Take care of the 30 percent first, or whatever percentage you can start your plan with. Take care of the stuff off the top first and learn to live off the rest. Make your investments, whatever size, before you pay your bills. Give to charity before you buy the extra things you want.

A man I know has an MBA (Master of Business Administration) from Harvard and an engineering degree from MIT (Massachusetts Institute of Technology). Smart guy, semiretired now, and doing what he likes best—teaching. He teaches college courses in economics and business planning. But when he teaches economics, he also teaches personal economics. He starts his classes saying, "Decide how you want to live now versus how long you want to work." This means if you want to spend everything you make now, you'll have to work longer and harder. But if you start investing in your financial future now, you'll have the choice between retiring early, or traveling more, or continuing your career, or starting a new career later in life. Once again, it all comes down to choices. Think tomorrow today and live better tomorrow.

Think tomorrow today and live better tomorrow.

Plan your debt just as carefully as you plan your fortune.

Here's the next thing to think of when you're planning your economic future: *be careful with your credit cards*. Selling money is big business. You probably get invitations in the mail to sign up for a new credit card several times a month. Having a credit card is important. Especially if you travel, it's safer and easier to track than cash. But be careful—when you buy something with a little piece of plastic, you don't feel the effect until you get the bill. Make sure that whatever you buy, you're still happy with your purchase after you get the bill.

And be careful with credit—it's the easiest way to get into debt. Go into debt strategically, not habitually. If your business is high risk, if you're an entrepreneur whose career requires a great deal of risk and a great deal of strategic debt, keep the debt in your business and out of your personal life. I know this one's hard too because for most entrepreneurs looking for capital, the lender requires you guarantee the debt personally. So plan your debt just as you plan your fortune.

Here's another point to remember in becoming financially independent: *it's hard to get rich fast; it's easy to get rich slowly.* The 70, 10, 10, and 10, or whatever percentages you're working with, doesn't happen overnight. With conservative investments, it takes a while to see increases. It takes discipline to keep adding value to your future a little every month. It takes time to build your fortune, your financial independence. There's a saying about investing: "Time, not timing." It takes time. Now if playing the stock market is what you do, then you know that timing is a whole other ball game. But for the average person, it takes time to acquire wealth.

A study was done a while back that analyzed stock market investments. The study took two scenarios into consideration. The first one took place over 40 years. In the first scenario, stocks were bought at the very worst possible time and sold at the very worst possible time—bought high and sold low. And after 40 years, the average return was around 10 percent. Scenario one dealt with *time*.

In the second scenario, stocks were analyzed over a 10-year period. The second scenario dealt with *timing*. Stocks were purchased at the best possible time and sold at the best possible time. After 10 years, the average return was around 10 percent.

Be patient in building your financial independence. It will come in small steps at a time, little advantages after little advantages. It's hard to be patient, but it's just like building your ambition and achieving your goals: it happens one step at a time.

And what if patience has nothing to do with building financial independence? What about those trust fund babies who are handed their financial independence on a silver platter, never having to work a day in their lives? First car is a Porsche; first house, a mansion; first job is at daddy's company. What about the people born rich? Someone says, "It isn't fair that I'm working like crazy every day all my life. It just isn't fair. I'll never have that kind of money."

Well, some things in life aren't fair. But what does that have to do with you, really? If your goal is to have greater financial independence, start working harder and smarter on your goals, your own visions, and stop pondering what's fair and what isn't. Start examining what's keeping you back instead of what's keeping them ahead. Start looking at what you're doing. Start looking at *you* instead of *it*. There are plenty of stories and examples and experiences of people who began their careers destitute and had enough resolve to "do it until"—until they had more than they ever dreamed of having. Study the experiences of others who built their way to the top instead of those who were born there.

Inevitable Disappointments

What if you decide you want to be rich? What if you really followed the power of your ambition and your life started turning around? Well, aside from getting on the right track, increasing your earning potential, decreasing the percent you spend, increasing the percent you save, investing, giving to worthy causes, and aside from all the benefits of achieving, there will also come some disappointments.

One of the disappointments that comes from achieving all you can be is in the people who choose to remain right where they are. Friends and family may chastise you for your accomplishments. They will abandon you for trying to become better. They will remain behind and say, "Boy, he's forgotten us now that he lives so well." And they'll probably say more than that. They'll probably gather in their little group and say all sorts of things to justify their own mediocrity.

But remember, those who choose to stay behind have chosen their own path, an average path, the path of mediocrity. And those who have climbed above the crowd almost always wished they

185

could return to their earlier friends to embrace them in friendship and love and try to help them get out of their ruts, to share ideas of hope and inspiration, but it rarely happens. Jealousy builds a big wall, one that is almost impossible to break down.

So as you change, your life will change. Your friends will change. Your circle of influence will change. And that's part of achievement and ambition and success, an ever-changing process required to become the person worthy of reaching your goals.

The Risk Factor

There are many reasons why people don't build their ambition, strive to become better, be the best they can—many reasons, but it only takes one. We talked about many fears in a previous chapter and how to work to overcome them. But one fear we didn't talk about—risk.

Different professions call for different levels of risk. There's an old saying: "No risk, no reward." Maybe that's the case in life; I don't know. It's a personal decision, one you have to make regarding how much risk you're comfortable in taking with your life and your future and your money. It's a personal decision.

What I do know is that there are different types of ambition, and each has its own reward. The ambitions of a salesperson are different from the ambitions of a manager. The ambitions of a manager or an executive are different from the ambitions of an entrepreneur. The ambitions of an entrepreneur are different from the ambitions of an artist or a scientist or a teacher.

With different levels of ambition come different levels of risk and different levels of reward. Salespeople are probably more able to handle risk than managers and professionals. And the higher the risk, the higher their earning potential. Entrepreneurs are probably even more risk-oriented. They have to be. An entrepreneur's ambition must overpower the risk of losing it all in an attempt to gain their dream.

Your level of ambition may or may not be equated with your ability to take on risk. Most people can't deal with much failure to reach success. There are only a few people, even among the most ambitious, who have the tenacity, intestinal fortitude, and tolerance level to follow a risky ambition. Whatever the level of ambition, whatever the level of risk, there must always be the discipline to overcome the failures and see the end result, to keep trying *until*.

Jonas Salk kept working through his failures until—until he developed the polio vaccine. Whatever your level of ambition, keep doing it until you get there. The riskier the ambition, the greater need for stability in your personal life. If you have everything on the line in your business, make sure everything is in line at home. John D. Rockefeller was very frugal in his personal habits, but he was willing to take risks—big risks with investments in debts, risks that made his colleagues shutter. He lived from 1839 to 1937 and yet is still considered to be one of the wealthiest Americans and richest people in modern history. His is truly a rags-to-riches story.

So as you're developing your own plan for financial independence, as you're working toward the ideal of living off of 70 percent of what you make, remember the first step is to define a plan. It may not be ideal, but you're taking the first steps.

And when you follow your plan, the money you put away today will help you build your financial independence tomorrow. And with financial independence—the result of your ambition, the reward of your ambition—with financial independence comes freedom like you've never known before, freedom and options to live where you want to live, to do what you want to do, to go where you want to go, to drive what you want to drive, to support the causes you want to support.

With financial independence comes the freedom of choice. It's okay to be rich. It's okay to be wealthy. It's okay to be successful, as long as it's at the service of others, not at their expense.

10

THE SUCCESS– FAILURE LINK

Success is the steady progress toward your own personal goals—goals designed by you with a plan implemented by you. Your goals, your philosophy, your plan. If success is the steady progress toward your own personal goals, what then is failure? Is failure working on a project that ended with poor results? No, of course not. Is failure launching a new product that failed miserably in the marketplace? No, of course not. Is failure doing the best you possibly can with your kids and having them disappoint you in a very personal way? No, of course not.

There's no failure in pouring your heart and soul and energy into something that didn't work. Rather, failure is not trying at all. If success is the steady progress toward your own personal goals, then failure is no progress at all—none, not even trying. Success and failure are always linked together. Success and failure are always linked to ambition. And let's remember: *success is doing; failure is not doing.* It's that simple.

Failure is not trying at all.

Tom Peters, world-renowned author and management expert, said, "There is only one way to be in serious trouble today, and that is not to be trying, not to be failing, not to be stretching yourself." Success is a doing; you have to actually do it. Activity is high priority in the life process to try and get maximum benefit out of what we have available: our resources, our skills, our knowledge, and our talents. Success is a doing that tries to get maximum benefit out of what we have available.

Benjamin Disraeli, former prime minister of England, said, "Nothing can resist a human will that will stake even its existence on its stated purpose." What a powerful set of words.

We've already talked about resolve, "doing it until," but here's what else resolve says. Resolve says, "I will." The formula for disaster: could, should, won't. The formula for fortune: can, do, will. "I can, I do, and I will." Two of the most powerful words in the language: *I will.*

Someone says, "I will climb the mountain."

They say, "It's too high. It's too difficult. It's too rocky. It's never been done before."

The person says, "Hey, it's my mountain. I'll climb it. Pretty soon you'll see me waving from the top or dead on the side because I'm not coming back until I've done it." Powerful.

There are several studies that show the greatest achievers aren't those who failed the least. No, the greatest achievers are those least frightened of failure. They're willing to take on the challenge without the guarantee of success, seeing the end but not sure when it will be or where it will be.

Although success and failure go hand in hand, many people have a problem with failure. They think it's a bad word, has a bad connotation. They don't see it as a stepping-stone; they see it as an end result. Quite often, success requires failure—sometimes many failures. In every scientific discovery, there were dozens or hundreds of failures before one success. Without failure, opportunity cannot be created. Without failure, there can be no success. But what is the measure of success? How do you know if you're successful—really successful? How do you know, especially when your success could be so vastly different from someone else's success?

How to Measure Success

You measure success by results, making measurable progress in reasonable time. That's all life asks. So you have to be reasonable with time. Don't be unreasonable with time, parent. Don't be unreasonable with time, manager, broker, business associate. Have patience. You can't ask somebody every five minutes, "How are you doing now?" That's too soon. The colleague says, "I haven't left the building yet. Give me a break." So if five minutes is too soon to ask, five years is what? Too long and too late.

So what is a reasonable time to ask for results as a measure of progress? At the end of the day. Don't allow more than a day to go by without making progress—writing some letters, having a conversation with your teenager. Don't postpone the important more than a day. On the job there are projects you have to get done within a day. Regarding your health disciplines, you have daily requisites. You can't say, "Well, I'll eat nine apples ten days from now." No, it's an apple a day. Some things you have to get done within a day. At five minutes to midnight, you realize you haven't eaten your daily apple—munch away and get it done.

The next reasonable time is a week. Some things you have to get done within a week. A week is a good chunk of time. Don't let more than a week go by without measuring to see how you're doing, what progress you've made.

John joins a small sales company on Monday. He's supposed to make ten calls the first week just to get acquainted out in the marketplace. Would it be legitimate to call John in on Friday and ask, "How many calls did you make?" Yes, that's a legitimate amount of time to ask for a measurable amount of progress. He knew he was supposed to make ten calls by the end of the week, by close of business Friday.

"How many calls did you make, John?"

John starts with a story.

You say, "John, I don't need a story. I just need a number."

Numbers tell us the whole story. On us personally, the numbers tell the whole story. Success is a numbers game.

There are three important questions to ask yourself in this area:

1. How much money have you saved and invested during your career?

2. In the last 90 days, how many books have you read to invest in the miracle of your mind, to give you ideas to ponder, to help fashion your future with meticulous care?

3. In the last six months, how many classes have you taken to improve your skills or develop new skills for your future and your family?

To measure success, you have to make progress in reasonable time. You have to look at the numbers and see how you're doing. How often should you weigh a new baby? Next spring, next month? No, you can't wait until next spring or even next month. It's necessary to weigh the child once a week to see whether the baby is gaining weight or losing weight, ensuring healthy growth.

How often should you check the corporation's accounts to see if it's healthy or not? Someone says, "Well, in a couple of years we'll get all the accounts together." No, you'll be out of business by then. In Las Vegas, the big gambling houses put together a financial statement to see where they are several times a day. Why? So much is happening, so keeping strict accounts is vital. Sometimes in business you can't wait until midnight, you can't wait until tomorrow—you have to know the numbers.

Be responsible for the set of your own sail. Leave it to no one else but yourself, and learn to refine the numbers for yourself.

How many pounds should you weigh at age 50?

John says, "Well, I have big bones."

Well, we'll give him 10 pounds for big bones, but when he is 25–30 pounds overweight, we have to turn on the caution light at home and at the office. Someone wonders, "What's that flashing caution light?" Oh, that's because John is overweight 30 pounds and we want to warn him. At 40 pounds the flashing red light comes on at home and at the office. Then at 50 pounds the siren goes off and he's on the way to the hospital facing a serious health issue.

Numbers are important.

Take Charge

I'm asking you to take charge of and be responsible for your life, your health, your decisions. Don't just drift along with the crowd, with those who don't care—don't care to be responsible about the numbers, meticulous about the numbers. Some numbers should be coming down, like the ones on your bathroom scale, and some numbers should be going up, like the number of books in your library.

Don't be satisfied until you've looked at and seriously considered all your numbers. Don't wait for somebody to come along and hold you accountable. What if nobody comes along? You have to be responsible yourself. Results are the name of the game. Let's check the numbers. Don't be satisfied with anything less than the best of numbers.

For example, how many times have you hugged your spouse and kids in the last few days? How many times have you said "no" to dessert over the past several meals? How many times have you said "thank you" to your project workmates for their effort? How many times have you met your sales goals in the past three months? How many times has your employer called you in to congratulate you for your work?

An interesting story: Jesus walked along one day and saw a fig tree. And as Jesus looked suspiciously at this fig tree, He said to His disciples, "Does that fig tree have any figs?" Do you think that's an important question? For a fig tree, it's an all-important question. "Does it have any figs?" His disciples said, "No, sir. Of all the trees you were to pick, this particular fig tree does not have any figs." The story says Jesus lost His cool—one of the few times. Why? I think to make a point. A fig tree without figs is unacceptable. Then Jesus said, "If that fig tree doesn't have any figs, I suggest you promptly take it out." And He added, "Why let it take up the ground?" So you have to get all your people together every once in a while and say, "Today we're counting the figs." Why? To see who gets to stay and who needs to go.

Help Others to Help Yourself

What if your results are not that good right now? What if you're going through some tough times and aren't quite sure what to do next? I speak at seminars and lectures and write books and audio programs so I can attend them all myself, read it again myself, listen again, which encourages, motivates, and increases my numbers. I don't do it just to hear myself talk or for the money. I do it because the teacher always receives the greatest lessons when he or she teaches others.

What's the best way out of a blue mood? Talk somebody else through theirs. What's the best way out of a mental energy slump? Talk somebody else through theirs. What's the best way to start solving your own problems? Talk to somebody else about theirs. Why? Because when you talk someone through their blue mood or their mental slump or their problem, you will hear yourself say amazing things. You'll hear all the knowledge that you've gathered come out to help another person. And it will ultimately help you by hearing it again. Trust me, it just works that way.

It's often easier to tap our resources for someone else than it is to tap them for ourselves. Sometimes defeat is the best beginning. Why? Well, for one, if you're at the very bottom, there's only one way to go—up. But more importantly, if you're flat on your back mentally and financially, you will usually become sufficiently disgusted to reach way down deep inside yourself and pull out miracles, pull out talents, pull out abilities, and pull out desires and determination.

The teacher receives the greatest lessons when teaching others.

From Disgust to Determination

When you're flat broke or flat miserable, you will eventually become so disgusted that you will pull out the basic essential required to make everything better—change. In the face of adversity, situations begin to change—you begin to change. With enough disgust, desire, and determination to change your life, you'll say, "I've had it. Enough of this. No more. Never again." And then there's where the miracle begins. These thoughts and words really rattle the power of time and fate and circumstances and the power of ambition.

And when time and fate and circumstances and the power of ambition all get together, you will be on your way up! Resolve, inspiration, and determination will blast through disgust and open wide doors and windows of opportunities just waiting for you to engage.

But a lot of people don't change themselves; they wait for change, circumstances to change, the government to change, life to change. What does waiting do? Not much. These unfortunate folks accept their defeats and wallow in their self-pity. Why? Because they refuse to take control of the situation. They refuse to take control of their life, their career, their health, their relationships, their finances. They refuse to take control and take responsibility and get sufficiently disgusted enough to change it.

Your present situation is a temporary condition, which will pass if you grasp for a new beginning.

If you are disgusted, if you are making changes, if you are in the middle of your own personal slump, I have some parting but important words to offer you: Your present condition is temporary. You will rebound from a seeming failure to success.

Somebody once suggested to me, about a failure, that I should tell myself, "This too shall pass." I firmly believe that we are only given as much as we can handle—as much negativity, as much failure, as much disappointment. So I tell you, "This too shall pass if you grasp for a new beginning, if you pull yourself up and move back into the world with a plan."

So as foolish as it might sound, be thankful for your current limitations or failures, as they are building blocks from which to create greatness. You can go where you want to go. You can do what you want to do. You can become what you want to become. You can do it all starting now, starting right where you are.

Limitations or failures are building blocks from which to create greatness.

A father talks about his daughter, who has gone through some pretty tough times. While most parents would be frantic about the circumstances, this man just smiles and says that his daughter is like a frog in a jar of cream. She keeps kicking and kicking and kicking, and pretty soon the milk will turn into a lump of butter and she'll be able to jump out. That's an interesting way to look at it—an interesting illustration of tenacity—and that's how it works.

You have to keep trying and trying and trying. You have to have enough resolve to *do it until*. So be grateful for adversity, and make it work for you, not against you. Make your failures stepping-stones into a successful future. Give birth to great opportunity, not prolonged agony. Make your disgust lead to inspiration, not depression. The world will willingly sit by and let you wallow in your sorrows until you die broke and alone. The world will also step aside and let you by when you choose to keep walking forward toward achieving your goals.

Once you decide that your present situation is only temporary, once you decide to get back on your feet and make your mark, the world will watch you go by. It doesn't care which path you choose. It won't make you stop here or there. The world doesn't really care, so you have to. You have to care enough about yourself to give a run at adventure.

Your Challenge

Keep your eyes firmly on achievement, on the power of your ambition, and don't merely exist in self-pity. Commit yourself to excellence. And remember, it is your challenge—your own personal challenge—to use all your gifts, and skills, and talents, and knowledge to succeed.

Now here's another thought for you. It's a big thought that can make all the difference in the world: *success is what you attract by the person you become*. Once I understood that, I changed my whole method of operation. Success is not something you pursue. What you pursue usually eludes you like a butterfly, something you go after that you can't catch. Success is something you attract like a magnet by the person you become.

Success is what you attract by the person you become.

To attract attractive people, you must be attractive. To attract powerful people, you must be powerful. To attract committed people, you must be committed. Instead of going to work on other people, trying to change them, get to work on yourself. Work harder on yourself than you work on the job. And if you become, you can attract. The whole key is to make yourself valuable. The key is to make yourself attractive. The key is to make yourself skillful, competent, willing, powerful, unique, sophisticated, cultured, able to manage, in control, and healthy.

The whole key to a wonderful future is personal development, because the greatest gift you can give is your self-investment in becoming the best person you can be, were designed to be. If you become ten times wiser, ten times stronger, ten times more competent, think of what that will do for your success. When you grow, think of what that will do for your future. Self-development earns success. Self-investment earns respect. And the only way to make a better and better and better investment in your future is to become better, and stronger, and wiser, and more competent. And the more attractive you become, the more attractive you are. And the more attractive you are, the more you attract success. Self-development and self-investment attract success. That's powerful.

Now here's what would be pitiful: if your income grew and you didn't grow mentally, physically, or spiritually. If your income takes some jumps and you haven't grown enough to know how to manage your larger income, it will eventually fade away. Somebody said, "If someone hands you a million dollars, best you become a millionaire so you get to keep the money." Success won't hang around an incompetent person. That's the problem with winning the lottery—the lack of self-development to be able to master it and keep it. The fortune is bigger than the person, rather than the person being bigger than the fortune. If you're a parent, use that as a challenge to grow personally. Use the challenge of parenting to grow; see what you can become.

Reach with Power and Wisdom and Love

An ancient writer wrote that God's arm is not short; He can reach out to all of us. Shouldn't that be said of every father, of every mother—that they can reach all of their children with wisdom and power and love? The only way you can become that kind of parent—the only way you can keep up that process—is by personal development; by becoming better, stronger, and wiser than you are. As your children grow, you grow—your power grows, your influence grows, your wisdom grows, your command of the language grows.

The same is true in the workplace or your business. It can be a challenge to be involved in a situation that makes you grow. But when you make wise decisions, your career, business, reputation, and all round you will keep growing your character to be bigger than your fortune. If a certain situation is failing, keep growing beyond it until you're bigger than the problem. Keep growing, keep becoming, keep *doing it until*.

Two Important Qualities

There are two qualities that can increase your chances of success: *patience* and *persistence*.

Patience is learning to handle the passing of time. When you have an appetite for success and start going for it, you have to learn to handle the passing of time, because it takes time to build a corporate work of art. It takes time to build a symphony orchestra with flawless music and harmony that sends you on flights of ecstasy to be remembered long after the orchestra has shut down and the lights have gone out.

It takes time to put harmony together. It takes time to build a life. It takes time to build an enterprise. It takes time to get through school. It takes time to develop and grow. So give your enterprise time; give your business time. If you're in management, give your people time. If you're a parent, give your kids time. Don't be too short, too quick; give them time—not unlimited time, but time enough.

The ultimate challenge is to have patience with yourself. It takes time to make changes in habit and discipline. It takes time to correct old errors in judgment and to finally give up old blame and pick up new responsibility.

It took me some time. I used to blame the government, and blame taxes, and blame the company, and blame the marketplace. It took me a long time to give all that up. That was a pretty comfortable list to explain my empty bank account, pennies in my pocket, nothing in the bank, not doing well, embarrassed by my situation. It took time to give that up and only blame myself. That took a while.

Being persistent means you keep doing it. Be persistent, be tenacious, keep *doing it until*. As long as you are patient and persistent, it's hard to elude success. As long as you maintain patience and persistence, tenacity, there's only one person— just one person—who will draw the line between success and failure—you. You need both patience and persistence together, because lack of patience is probably the worst enemy of ambition.

While your ambition keeps growing, keeps moving, keeps looking for new ways to succeed, impatience tends to grow frustrated. Impatience won't allow for persistence. Impatience wants to give up. Impatience calls discouragement and failure, but your ambition will not let you give up so easily. What others may call failure ambition calls a learning opportunity, a chance to make adjustments along the charted course to success. Ambition knows that the longer the achievement is in coming, the more valued it will be.

Six Aspects of Patience

Some examples to illustrate the six aspects of patience include:

1. Knowing when an opportunity is right and when more preparation is needed.

Let's say you're opening a restaurant specializing in fresh seafood. You're all excited to get going, get the money coming in instead of it all going out. You're all excited. So because you're all excited, you want to open early; your impatience gets the best of you.

And so you open before your scheduled grand opening. Customers start coming in. They're all excited about the new, great restaurant. And everybody wants fresh seafood. They're all ordering fresh seafood from the menu—and now you panic. You don't have any. You're not ready. The fresh seafood shipment won't come in for a week. Impatience has just killed the restaurant.

Now let's say you have a great new product that's scheduled to come out on the market in the next several months. Everything's going according to plan, so you start planning your ads, start planning big public relations events. You're so sure that it's going to happen that you set a date. The engineer told you that the product is not ready, but you're sure it will be. You start planning everything, invite lots of people—influential people, potential buyers of your product. You're so excited that you go ahead without the product actually being completed. Come the week of the grand unveiling, the engineer comes to you and says it still doesn't work. Your impatience just lost your credibility in the marketplace.

That's number one: Be patient and know the difference between when the opportunity is right and when more work needs to be done.

2. Remain alert even if opportunity doesn't come right away.

Make sure that your patience allows you to keep your eyes open and ready for opportunity. Keep looking; be patient.

3. Continually prepare for opportunities even if there is a delay.

Even if things aren't going just the way you think they should, keep your disappointments at bay and keep getting ready for opportunities. Be prepared—always be prepared. Don't let impatience allow you to give up.

4. Take little setbacks in stride.

Don't let small disappointments discourage you. Don't let the little successes delude you. Avoid the emotional rollercoaster that will always, always disrupt your plans.

5. If you have to wait on other people's decisions, be patient.

You can't control the decision-making abilities of others. You can't control their timing. If your project was to come up before the board in one meeting and time ran out and they moved your project to the top of the agenda for the next meeting, be patient. Don't be frustrated about what you have no control over.

6. Take a vacation from your ambition.

If you've been working day after day, week after week, month after month without a break, take a vacation from your ambition. Those patient and secure in their ambition know that the drive and ambition will still be there even after some time off. As a matter of fact, after a time of refreshment, your ambitious plans will have a stronger pull than ever when you return to it. Persistence is patience in action. Persistence is creative, always looking for new opportunities. Persistence is courageous; it doesn't give in to fear.

Persistence is patience in action—hopeful, positive, and cheerful.

Persistence is hopeful. It doesn't let discouragement through the door. Persistence is positive. It keeps your plans and your goals on track. And persistence is cheerful—not gloomy; cheerful. Persistence knows that gloom and depression and disappointments waste energy. Cheerfulness creates energy. Patience and persistence are both required for success.

207

Please remember that success and failure are intricately intertwined. Without failure, you can never appreciate success. And quite often, without failure, there will never be success.

11

MORE THAN YOUR AMBITION

You are more than your ambition. These are undoubtedly some of the most valuable words in this book about *The Power of Ambition.* You are more than your ambition. You can't serve your ambition. No, your ambition must serve you. If you serve your ambition, you become less than your ambition. If you don't allow your ambition to serve you, your ambition won't have any resources to pull from, to grow, to maintain. It won't have a reservoir of strength and discipline and ingenuity and creativity. If you serve your ambition, it will be weakened. There will be nothing to revive and replenish it.

So how do you make sure that your ambition is serving you?

Let's review the methods for building your ambition, the principles for building your ambition, the building blocks—the fundamental philosophies—that we must continue to work on so our ambition will continue to serve us, work for us.

Let's go through these one more time, because these building blocks help develop the foundation of good, strong ambition.

Principle 1: Positive self-direction

Positive self-direction says, "I know who I am. I know where I want to go. I am working on my plan to get there." In positive self-direction, you accumulate knowledge, and experiences, and feelings, and philosophies. You gather all that you can to help you decide where you want to go, how you want to get there, how to keep on track.

Principle 2: Self-reliance

Self-reliance is taking responsibility for your own life; taking full responsibility for whatever happens to you; taking the credit or the blame for the result of yesterday's activities; changing what's in your power to change; being responsible; working with others, yes, but doing all you can to bring the most value to the table, to the marketplace; being self-reliant, responsible.

Principle 3: Consistent self-discipline

This is one of the most powerful of the six principles and the one that will undoubtedly prevent you from living with the pain of regret. An ounce of discipline weighs far less than a ton of regret, the pain of regret. A little discipline every day will make all the difference in the world. It makes all the difference in your health. It makes all the difference in your wealth. It makes all the difference today. And this discipline—consistent self-discipline practiced at the daily level—will make all the difference in your tomorrows.

Principle 4: Self-enterprise

Self-enterprise is to keep your eyes open and your mind active, to recognize an opportunity and to grasp it, to consistently create opportunity, to be disciplined enough and prepared enough to take advantage of the opportunities around you. An enterprising attitude says, "Find out before action is taken. Do your homework. Do the research. Be prepared. Be resourceful. Do all you can in preparation of what will inevitably come to you, what you're preparing to come to you."

Principle 5: Working with others

The fifth principle of building your ambition is manifested by working with others; being able to share the spotlight; keeping your ego in your back pocket and giving others credit when

211

credit is due; caring enough about others to offer a kind word, a thoughtful gesture, a helping hand. Remember, it's hard to find a rich hermit. The next time you say the Pledge of Allegiance, notice that it starts with the word "I" and ends with "all." A country can't be built by one person. A company can't be built with one person. A family can't be built with one person. A friendship can't be built with one person. Each of us needs all of us to succeed. Each of us must learn to work with others to achieve our goals, to finish our tasks.

Principle 6: Self-appreciation

You must develop a strong appreciation for the conclusions that you have made; for the sail you have set; for the philosophies you have adopted; for your own methods, your own style, your own model of success. Remember that success is the steady progress toward your own personal goals, and self-appreciation is crucial in keeping you moving toward those goals.

So there you have a review of the six principles necessary to build your ambition.

In the previous chapters, we have also learned how to bring balance to our work and personal lives, to understand the rewards of ambition—that it's okay to be rich and wealthy—and to understand that success and failure are part of the same process. Through the consistent practice of everything covered in this book, you will begin to develop *three cornerstones of the ambitious life: focused concentration, resilience, and integrity.* By developing these traits, by incorporating them into your character deep within your very being, you will allow your ambition to serve you. You can direct your ambition to achieve even your wildest dreams. And you'll have the satisfaction of knowing you're on the right course.

Three Cornerstones

Together, these three cornerstones—focused concentration, resilience, integrity—bring stability to your ambition, stability which is the most valuable asset in the pursuit of achievement. We'll cover each of these—focused concentration, resilience, and integrity—in depth. But the key point here is that each of these cornerstones is cultivated only through the practice of the six principles of building your ambition. The six principles, worked on consistently and simultaneously, will develop these three traits in your character.

1. Focused concentration

We talked about this topic in the time management section, but the key to building your ambition, keeping on track with all of the principles, is focused concentration. You have to zero in. You have to identify your target. Let nothing stand in your way. You have to keep your eye on the target until you've released the arrow. Let nothing capture your attention unless it's in the best interest of your ambition. Let not an obstacle come before you without getting around it, going over it, going under it, trying a different path until you get there.

Concentration in sports is crucial. The consummate professional, on the field or on the court, won't hear the cheering crowd. Their concentration keeps all noise and clutter at bay. They have one thing in mind—moving the ball. You have to have only one thing in mind: keeping on track, closing out all the noise and the clutter that gets in your way, going around all the obstacles of negativity and influence. In a tennis match, how long does it take for an opponent to return the ball? Not very long. And what if you lose your concentration? The game is over. One little slip

213

of concentration—just that fast—one little slip of concentration, and your opponent puts the ball by your feet and there goes the tennis match.

In a major presentation, just lose your concentration for a flash of a second and you could lose it all—all the hard work, all the long hours, all the preparation. All the momentum building to that crucial presentation could be gone. If you don't keep your concentration focused, if you don't watch your audience, if you don't keep your mind on what you're doing, if you aren't focused on the task at hand, it could slip right on by you.

Wherever you are, be there.

Wherever you are, be there. Whatever you're supposed to be doing for the moment, do it. You can't be thinking of everything you have to do at one time all the time. You have to concentrate on just one thing at a time—one project, one job. You have to take it one task at a time and complete it. Do what you've set out to do. Keep your mind only on that one task. Why? If you don't, you won't accomplish anything.

Concentration takes a lot of discipline—to demand privacy, to keep the "Do Not Disturb" sign on your door while you're in the middle of an important job. It takes a lot of discipline not to answer the phone every time it rings at home. That's why they make voicemail and answering machines, emails, and texts—so you don't have to answer every time. Your family will appreciate an uninterrupted dinner hour. Your night work will get done a whole lot faster. Concentrate on the work at hand and demand of yourself the discipline to stay focused.

If you have a long list of things to get done within a day, do the toughest ones while your concentration is at its peak. If you're a morning person, get the job done in the morning. Don't wait until the evening when your energy is all spent. No, do the jobs that need the most concentration when your body is best able to handle them. If you're a night person, save those tough jobs for the night, not in the morning when you have cobwebs in your brain. Learn your body's rhythms, and do the jobs that need the most concentration when you're able to do them best.

When you're at work, be at work. When you're in a conference, be in that conference. When you're at your kid's school play or soccer game or dance recital, be there. Don't let your mind wander. Stay focused on the task at hand or the company you're with. Don't let your mind wander during conversations—you never know what important points you may miss. Stay focused. Stay true to where you are and what you're doing. Use your discipline to keep your mind in line.

When you recognize the need to concentrate more and you discipline yourself to stay focused, it will come easier and easier. Focused concentration can be learned and can become a habit. If you work on it a little every day, the easier it comes and the less energy you will waste on making your mind mind you. The number one cornerstone of an ambitious person is focused concentration. Make your mind pay attention. Discipline yourself to be where you are. Work at work and play at play; don't mix the two. Concentrate. Give your job the attention it deserves. Give your family the attention they deserve. Give your colleagues the attention they deserve.

2. Resilience

Resilience is the ability to return to the original form after being bent or being stretched or compressed—that's the dictionary's definition of resilience—the ability to readily recover from illness or depression or adversity. Resilience is being able to withstand setbacks, broken hearts and broken dreams, financial crisis, loss of loved ones, loss of enterprise, and loss of health. How would you handle life if you lost everything you had today? What would your next step be? How long would you be depressed and upset and angry? What would it take for you to pull yourself up and start all over again? How resilient are you? Could you handle it? Could you learn from all your disappointments and start all over again? What would it take?

First, it would take a lot of self-discipline. It would take a lot of positive self-talk to muster up the energy to begin again. It would take a lot of concentration to block out the noise and the clutter of all the negative voices trying to get through—your negative voices and the negative voices of others around you. It would take a lot of discipline to balance the fear and anxiety with the knowing that if you did it once, you can do it all over again.

It would also take a lot of self-reliance. Whether your losses had anything to do with you or not, your future success has everything to do with you. It would take a lot of self-reliance to avoid blame. What's happened has happened. You would need to get on with your life and begin again. It would also take a lot of faith and trust in God to move ahead. If you lost everything tomorrow and were gathering all the courage to try again, it would take a lot of self-appreciation, knowing that you have the skills and the talent and the strength to do it one more time.

Resilience is the ability to bounce back from adversity.

Resilience is the ability to bounce back from adversity, no matter how large or how small. What if you lose one of your biggest clients, accounts comprising over 25 percent of your gross revenues? Losing this client is going to hurt financially and emotionally. Losing this client is going to negatively affect things for a while. The first thing you do is to figure out why you lost this business. What role did you play? What part are you responsible for?

You just can't rant and rave around the office, yelling and screaming at everyone around you. Even if it was the wrongdoing of someone else, don't act unprofessionally. You'll lose respect, which is hard to regain once you've lost it—the respect of those you work with, trusted colleagues, valuable support people. You must approach the situation rationally and figure out how to bounce back from your loss. You have to evaluate the situation and then start a plan to recapture the lost business, increase your market share with other businesses, network with associates to bring in a similar client or a larger one.

Don't sit back and dwell on what happened; get back at it.

Don't sit back and dwell on what's happened. No, you have to get back into the marketplace and recapture what's been taken from you. Get back at it and replace what's gone.

Maybe your loss is a personal loss: death of a loved one, divorce, loss of a very special friendship. If your loss is a deeply personal one, you must approach the situation a little differently. You must be patient with yourself and give yourself time—time to grieve, time to mourn, time to regroup. The five stages we go through in loss—be it death of a loved one, death of a rela-tionship, or death of an enterprise—are beautifully defined in the book *On Death and Dying,* written by Elisabeth Kübler-Ross. If the death is a literal one or a figurative one, the stages are the same: denial, anger, bargaining, depression, and acceptance. And only by going through these stages and reaching acceptance can we rebound and begin again.

It said that children are often more resilient than adults. Why? Well, maybe it's because they don't evaluate their current situations based on past experiences. They approach them in a fresh way, a new way. And in their own minds, they deal with loss much better than adults. Children who grow up in the unfortunate circumstances of poverty or abuse or neglect and become successful are known as "dandelion children" because if they can succeed and prosper with terrible conditions, they can grow anywhere. It's important to be more like a dandelion child—to be able to grow and prosper and succeed despite our current conditions, to be able to grow and prosper and succeed despite our losses, to be resilient.

Cultivating a resilient character turns what others would call failure into success. A resilient person won't give up. A resilient person will, in spite of all obstacles and setbacks, keep *doing it until.*

In the book *The Resilient Self,* Steven and Sybil Wolin have studied the characteristics of resilience and found seven key skills that comprise it.

To build a resilient character, you must have (1) insight, the ability to ask tough questions of yourself and be honest with your answers. If you had something to do with your loss, be honest and responsible for it.

(2) Resilience is independent. A resilient person counts only on themselves to bounce back into life.

(3) Although resilience is independent, it's also tied to others. The more people you are responsible to, the greater the motivation to begin again. The stronger the reason, the stronger the action.

(4) Another component of resilience is initiative, the ability to take charge of the situation, the ability to take charge of the problem, the ability to stand up and do whatever is necessary to get back on course.

(5) A resilient person is creative, being able to look at the situation and creatively determine the best way out, to look for solutions, to be enterprising in your approach toward starting over.

(6) A resilient person has a sense of humor. They may cry until they start laughing, but a sense of humor is so important when turning your life around. You have to take your ambition seriously, and you have to take yourself seriously; but you've also got to be able to laugh at yourself sometimes, your situation. Somebody says, "You'll look back on this and laugh someday." Well, maybe today is the day to start.

(7) A resilient person has a moral character. Whatever you do to get back on your feet—whatever you do to bounce back into life—make sure it's moral. Make sure that your upcoming success is at the service of others, not at the expense of others. I have made this point several times throughout this book because it's so important. Success, if it is yours to keep, must be at the service of others.

3. Integrity

The three cornerstones for an ambitious life are concentration, resilience, and integrity. Integrity is adhering to the moral principles of life. Integrity is doing things with honor. Integrity is honesty. Without integrity, ambition loses its unifying focus that comes from integrated goals, from really knowing what you want. Integrity says, "I wish to pay a fair price for value. Getting something for nothing makes nothing of me. Getting it cheap makes me cheap." Truly, this is self-interest, and it's also integrity. Why? For what it will make of me, for what paying for it will make of me. By paying, you have the integrity not to take advantage of others.

You hear of greedy people boasting about the great deal they just got, the best value, how they negotiated the price down to nothing, how they nickel-and-dimed the other person out of making a profit. Integrity won't let you do that. We all shop for the greatest value at the best price, but not at the expense of others, not when your great deal cheated someone out of their profit.

When you hire someone to do a job, you have to pay a fair price, a fair value for someone else to do the work for you. If you don't, they will never work for you again. No one wants to work long, hard hours to make you look good and not get compensated for it. Your integrity won't allow that to happen. Pay an honest price for an honest value. Make it good for everybody involved. Don't be cheap; be fair. Your integrity is on the line, not just a few bucks—your integrity.

If I want something badly enough, I have to earn it, I have to pay for it. Why? Because of what paying for it will make of me. And if I wish to have more, I must become more. I must earn more. And how much should you earn? As much as you possibly can. You must always strive to do all you possibly can. The essence of life is growth—doing, becoming, striving, growing, achieving. Be like the tree that grows as high as it can. Be like the bird that soars as high as it can. Be like the flowers that bloom as much as they can. Whatever course you set your sail to, do as much as you can to get there. That concept is part of integrity. Honestly do all you can in pursuit of what you want, in pursuit of what you'll become; and whatever you sign up for, finish it.

The essence of life is growth—doing, becoming, striving, growing, achieving.

Here's a great story about integrity. Paraphrasing the apostle Paul, he said he was going away and the reputation he was leaving behind—what he wanted people to say about him—was first, "I fought a good fight." Let that be your reputation. You fought a good fight. You kept out the ideology that wanted to capture your children, threatened every enemy that ever threatened you, fought like a parent protecting children in the home front. You fought a good fight. And whether or not you won, at least let your reputation be that you fought a good fight: fought for your rights, fought for the game, you fought for your integrity, you fought for honesty, you fought for success. You didn't leave any energy unspent. You fought. The major key to have success of any kind—you have to leave this reputation behind. "I've fought a good fight." Wow.

The second thing Paul hoped people would say after he left was that he finished the task. "I stayed until it was done. They gave me a task, and I finished it. I didn't leave it half done. I never walked off the court in the third quarter; I stayed. I finished it." What a good reputation. Finish it. Finish your assignment. Finish the project. Finish the contract. Finish whatever you've signed up for.

The third thing he said: "I kept the faith." Boy, that's important. Keep faith with your family. Keep faith with your church. Keep faith with your enterprise, the group you belong to. We pledge our faith, our unwavering confidence in each other. Each of us pledge that to all of us. I wish for you to be in a group that has so much integrity that you want to be involved with people who pledge and keep your confidences.

"I fought a good fight, I finished the job, and I kept the faith."

The insurance company Allstate's slogan is "You're in good hands." That should be the reputation of all of us. Develop the reputation of good hands so that no matter where you go, you will represent your family, your company, and yourself well. Have integrity; honesty; success at the service of others, not at the expense of others—and at the end of the road, you can say, "I fought a good fight, I finished the job, and I kept the faith."

That last part, keeping the faith, is not that easy. What is part of the Master's prayer? "Lead us not into temptation, but deliver us from evil." Help us keep integrity in spite of the evil, in spite of going through the valley of the shadow of darkness, that we will not fear that evil will dislodge us from our integrity. Keep the faith of the office. Keep the faith of the company. Keep the faith of the family, of your spouse, and of your children. Keep the faith of the church. Keep the faith of the community.

Represent Yourself Well

Wherever you go, represent your family well. Wherever you go, represent your group well. Wherever you go, represent your colleagues well. Let part of the bond of friendship be that wherever you are, you will represent well. Wow. What a thing to be able to say: "I fought a good fight, I finished the course, and I kept the faith." And here's how Paul wrapped it up: "I understand now there's a crown waiting for me, and I deserve it." Isn't that great? "I hear they have a trophy for me, and guess what? I deserve it." What a magnificent story to leave behind. "I fought a good fight, I finished the job, I kept the faith, and I deserve the crown." Remarkable!

Others you associate with may not have the ambition or the integrity to leave such a legacy behind, but you do. In the challenge of building your ambition and stepping up to the opportunity of giving someone else light and direction and refinement of thought and character—in all of this—let everybody else lead small lives if that is their choice, but not you. Let everybody else cry over small hurts, but not you. Let everybody else argue over nonessentials, but not you.

You deal in things that matter, the larger challenge, the larger opportunity. Go for the challenge and the responsibility of being the absolute best you can—of doing your best; of creating your best; of being the best person, the best friend, the best spouse, the best parent, the best colleague.

Go for the challenge and the responsibility of being the absolute best you can.

As you begin to understand and apply all of the principles in building your ambition, remember that ambition is an eager desire to achieve, to be successful at the service of others; an eager desire to get ahead in life, to do more for your family, to prosper in health and wealth and relationships. As you're building and using your power of ambition to inspire and fuel your achievement, when you realize that you are more than your ambition, and when you let your ambition serve you, you will develop greater concentration, greater resilience, and greater integrity.

These three aspects will inspire more ambition—ambition that stems from the need to be true and to express your best innermost self. And with focused concentration, resilience, and integrity in your character working for you, you are constantly inspiring the ambitious part of your nature to reach to greater and greater heights.

One of the most challenging experiences in life is seeing what you can do to help someone else. And one of the greatest thrills in life is being able to invest life into life.

I wish for you the ultimate understanding of your own power. I wish for you heightened ambition, achievement, and influence. I wish for you treasures of the soul, and of the spirit, and of the mind, and of the wallet. And hopefully what I have shared has given you extra perception in sharpening your skills and making your life unique.

Let the power of your ambition serve you, lead you to greatness, and motivate you to go and touch somebody else.

About the Author

For more than 40 years, Jim Rohn honed his craft like a skilled artist—helping people the world over sculpt life strategies that expanded their imagination of what is possible. Those who had the privilege of hearing him speak can attest to the elegance and common sense of his material. It is no coincidence, then, that he is still widely regarded as one of the most influential thinkers of our time and thought of by many as a national treasure. He authored countless books and audio and video programs and helped motivate and shape an entire generation of personal development trainers and hundreds of executives from America's top corporations.

Jim Rohn shared his message with more than 6,000 audiences and over 5 million people worldwide. He received numerous industry awards, including the coveted National Speakers Association CPAE Award and the Master of Influence Award. Jim's philosophies and influence continue to have worldwide impact.

Jim focused on the fundamentals of human behavior that most affect personal and business performance. His is the standard to which those who seek to teach and inspire others are compared. He possessed the unique ability to bring extraordinary insights to ordinary principles and events, and the combination of his substance and style still captures the imagination of those who hear or read his words.